THE DECORATIVE
THIRTIES

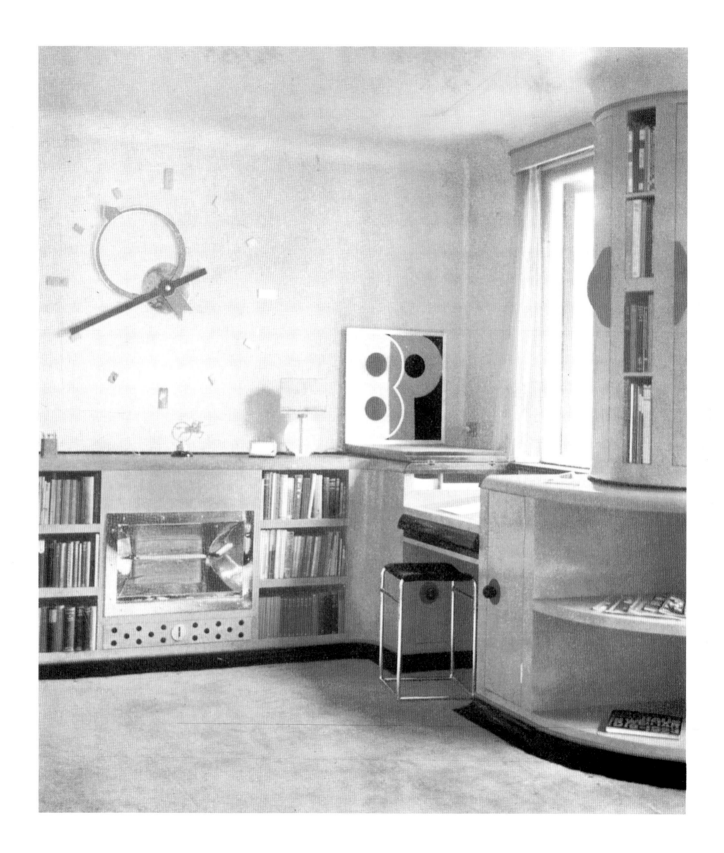

THE DECORATIVE THIRTIES

MARTIN BATTERSBY

Revised and edited by
PHILIPPE GARNER

THE HERBERT PRESS

ACKNOWLEDGMENTS

TO THE FIRST EDITION

My grateful thanks to all those who have racked their memories for first-hand information about their work and experiences during the thirties and in particular to Raoh Schorr; Miss Brown; Frederick Mayor, who allowed me to consult his records of the Mayor Gallery; Herman Schrijver, whose reminiscences of both decorators and clients in the thirties are diverting but, alas, too often unrepeatable; Oliver Messel; Mrs Reco Capey and Mrs Curtis Moffat, each of whom placed her husband's records at my disposal; Mr and Mrs Digby Morton; and Winnafreda, Countess of Portarlington. I must also thank Jonathan Joseph of Boston who so kindly searched for and sent me copies of contemporary magazines; Anne Urquhart for photographs of work done by Smyth, Urquhart and Marckwald; PEL, Best and Lloyd and The French Line for catalogues; Philip Dyer for help in tracing ballet photographs; the staff of Brighton Reference Library and the Director and Staff of Brighton Museum for their assistance in photographing pieces in the collection; and a special word of gratitude to Josephine Hickey for all her help in bringing order out of chaos.

Martin Battersby

PICTURE CREDITS AND ACKNOWLEDGMENTS

© ADAGP, Paris and DACS, London 1988: 88, 142, 160, 183 (*left*); Architects' Journal: 48, 51; Architectural Review: 52, 55, 56, 57, 58, 106; Artek: 90; Bauhaus-Archiv: 21, 26; BBC Hulton Picture Library: 30, 31, 189 (*bottom*); Brighton: Royal Pavilion Art Gallery and Museums: 9, 10, 124; Cartier: 185, 199 (*top*), 208; Art Institute of Chicago: 172; Cooper-Hewitt Museum of the Smithsonian Institution/Art Resource: 112, 113; © DACS 1988: 15, 111 (*left*), 158 (*top*), 167 (*bottom*), 168 (*bottom*), 174 (*bottom right*); © DEMART PRO ARTE BV 1988: 172, 180; Design Council: 125, 138, 143 (*top*); David Gill: 163; Angelo Hornak: 155, 157; Angelo Hornak/Trustees of Edward James: 176; Peter Jackson Collection: 202–3; John Jesse: 181 (*top*); David King Collection: 6; Kobal Collection: 216, 217, 218; Irina Laski: 181 (*bottom*); Raymond Mander and Joe Mitchenson Theatre Collection: 75; Millar and Harris: 54, 60, 71 (*both*), 74, 79, 80, 100 (*both*); Museum of Modern Art, New York: 174 (*top*); National Film Archive, London: 103, 214; National Trust: 154; Paul Newark's Western Americana: 146 (*left*); Norman Parkinson: 179; Peninsular and Orient Steam Navigation Co.: 46, 47; Rockwell Museum, Corning, New York: 130; Royal Commission for Historical Monuments, England: 219; Sotheby's London: 120, 159; Sotheby's London, Cecil Beaton Archive: 81, 170, 198 (*left*), 204, 209; Sotheby's New York: 194 (*both*); Tate Gallery Publications: 180; Theatre Museum, London: 167; Victoria and Albert Museum: 93 (*bottom*), 96 (*bottom*), 100 (*right*), 116, 147, 149, 200; Glynn Vivian Art Gallery and Museum, Swansea: 152.

All other illustrations are from private collections.

The author and publishers would also like to thank Anne-Marie Ehrlich for picture research, and Tim Imrie and Eileen Tweedy for special photography.

Opposite title page: Study designed by Rodney Thomas for Ashley Havinden in the early 1930s. The Modernist style is seen here in the clean lines, undecorated surfaces, and references such as the tubular steel stool and the strictly geometrical wall clock. A Bauhaus catalogue is displayed in self-conscious isolation on the lower right-hand shelf.

Chapter headings: Sketch of a rug design by Da Silva Bruhns, 1930.

First published 1971
Reprinted 1976

This revised edition first published 1988 by
The Herbert Press,
46 Northchurch Road,
London N1 4EJ

Original text © 1971 Martin Battersby
Introduction and revisions © 1988 Philippe Garner
Volume © 1988 John Calmann and King Ltd

British Library Cataloguing in Publication Data
Battersby, Martin
    The decorative thirties.—Rev. ed.
    1. Design, 1930–1940
    I. Title   II. Garner, Philippe
    745.4'442

    ISBN 0-906969-90-5

This book was designed and produced by
JOHN CALMANN AND KING LTD, LONDON

Designed by Richard Foenander
Typeset by Rowland Phototypesetting Ltd, England
Printed in Singapore by Toppan Ltd

CONTENTS

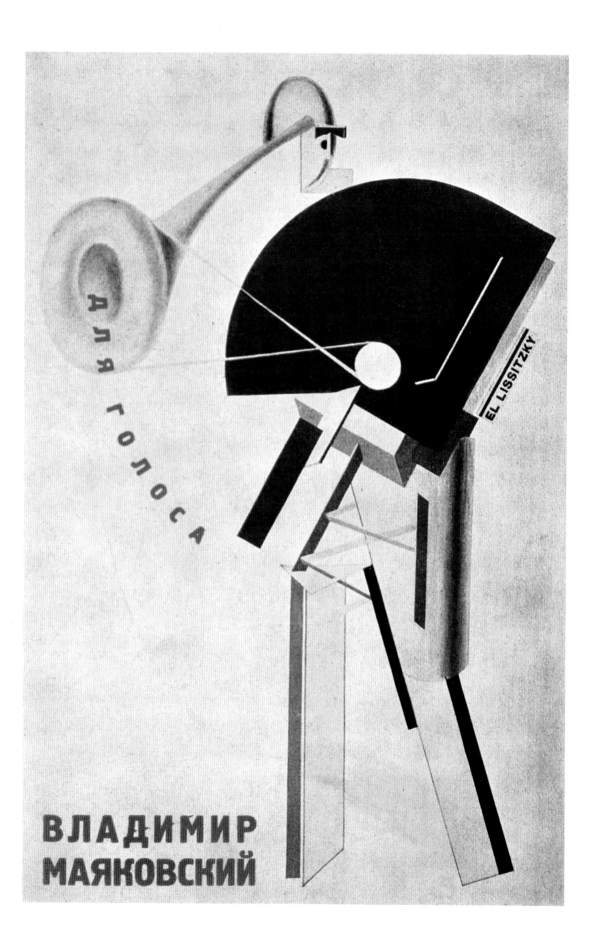

MARTIN BATTERSBY:
THE LITERATURE

T he simultaneous republication of the present work and its companion volume, *The Decorative Twenties*, presents an excellent opportunity to assess the influential role the two books have played and to analyse in some detail their significance within the bibliography of their subject.

A new preface to *The Decorative Twenties* provides a biography of Martin Battersby which sheds light on his background and credentials as a chronicler of the decorative arts of the period 1890–1939. This preface, to *The Decorative Thirties*, concentrates on Battersby's writings in the context of a bibliographic survey.

The study of these two facets, biographical and bibliographical, serves to emphasize the consistencies of viewpoint between the two books and the completeness with which, as companion volumes, they tell the story of the most significant aspects of the decorative arts in France, England and the United States in the crucial, formative years before the First World War and through the two subsequent decades. The term "decorative arts" is used advisedly and the full relevance of the books' titles should not be overlooked, for Battersby's concern was above all with the

history of style, most particularly as it evolved in the context of interior decoration, luxury artefacts and fashion.

A full study of the bibliography, both contemporary and retrospective, of the applied arts of these decades reveals the significance of the evolution of a new vision of design, allied to industrial and populist considerations. This was bound up with the progress of a theoretical debate on the concept of "pure" design which is at the very basis of the Modern movement. The roots of this movement can be identified in the impassioned fervour of revolutionary manifestos and journals. Modernist ideology, as applied primarily to architecture but no less passionately to the full infrastructure of the applied arts, can be traced through such landmark tracts as Walter Gropius's April 1919 Bauhaus Manifesto; its wild Italian precursor, Filippo Marinetti's Futurist Manifesto, published in February 1909; through such periodicals as *De Stijl*, published by a Dutch avant-garde group from late 1917, or Le Corbusier and Amédée Ozenfant's *L'Esprit Nouveau*, first published in 1920. Le Corbusier's theories were distilled in *Vers une Architecture* (1923), a seminal volume which set the tone of the Modernist vision, a vision which found less polemical, but nonetheless important, expression in such documents as the series of *Jahrbuch des Deutschen Werkbundes*, published by the Deutsche Werkbund, founded in 1907, or the 1930

Left: Title page designed by the Russian Constructivist El Lissitzky for the pamphlet containing Mayakovsky's poem "For the Voice", published in Berlin in 1923.

Right: The architect and designer Le Corbusier (1887–1965), photographed by Man Ray in about 1930.

Below: Le Corbusier's bedroom designed by himself in the early 1930s. When this photograph was published in *The Architectural Review* in 1935, the writer P. Morton Shand eulogized the "poet" in Corbusier, and "his uncanny gift of extracting ever fresh aesthetic values from old and new materials alike." Few readers can have agreed with him, considering the inconvenience of the height of the bed, the lack of privacy in the sanitary arrangements (the bidet was almost unknown in England at this time) and the general air of clinical discomfort.

Above: Martin Battersby in his flat at 36 Sussex Square, Brighton, in the early to mid 1960s. On the wall to the right is his portrait by Roy Little, and on the shelf are various Art Nouveau artefacts from his own collection, including glass and metalwork. The two sculptures are of Nijinsky.

survey *Die Sachlichkeit in der Modernen Kunst*, with an introduction by Henry van de Velde.

Ratification of the Modern Movement as the vanguard of a Darwinian progress towards a utopian ideal of design was to be provided by Professor Nikolaus Pevsner. His theories, first published in 1936 as *Pioneers of the Modern Movement* and subsequently revised and republished in 1960 as *Pioneers of Modern Design*, established a template for the study of architecture and the applied arts of the late nineteenth and early twentieth centuries. In recent years, however, Pevsner's orthodoxy has been regularly challenged.

Battersby makes no direct challenge, but his attitude is implicit. He acknowledges the ideologies of Modernism but is more intrigued by its stylistic aspects. Abstract theories of design are not his concern. His interest is in taste, his forte is the study of the minutiae of fashions in forms, motifs, materials and colours, their subtle evolutions and the personalities who influenced these evolutions. His respect for the influence of fashion on all aspects of design, even so-called functionalism, is well expressed in a revealing sentence in the chapter on "Art and Industry" in the present book. "Another fact", wrote Battersby, "that the enthusiasts of fitness for purpose tended to

forget is that an original piece of design, however theoretically functional that design may be, is still a reflection in some way or another of the time in which it is made and consequently governed by the laws of fashion."

Battersby's bibliographies and his own extensive library provide an instructive introduction to the contemporary source works on the decorative aspects of design in the first decades of the twentieth century. His library included runs, part runs and individual issues of various key periodicals, notably the British publications *The Studio*, pioneer of the genre, and *The Artist*; the French *Art et Décoration*, and several of the contemporary German magazines, including *Deutsche Kunst und Dekoration*, *Kunst Gewerbeblate*, and *Innen Dekoration*. This generation of journals followed a pattern established by *The Studio*, from its first publication in 1893, of integrating essays and reviews with illustrations, mostly halftone reproductions from photographs, a technique made possible by recent innovations in platemaking and printing processes.

The Studio served as a model for publishers internationally. The wealth of illustrated magazines on the fine and decorative arts which followed it provided a crucial mechanism for the dissemination and exchange of ideas and provide subsequent generations with a rich source of reference. *The Studio* published many special numbers on specific subjects. Battersby's library included issues on "The Graphic Arts of Great Britain" (1917), "The New Book Illustration in France" (1924), "Posters and their Designers" (1924), "Art and Publicity" (1925) and "Modern Publicity" (1931). These were complemented from 1906 by year books. Other British journals of note included *The Magazine of Art* and *The Architectural Review*, the latter referred to extensively by Battersby in *The Decorative Thirties*.

Two notable publishers in Germany deserve credit for their contributions in the sphere of the art journal. Alexander Koch, in the artists' colony at Darmstadt, was a publisher of considerable vision who played an influential, catalystic role. He was instrumental, through his publications, in introducing the English Arts and Crafts designers, and Charles Rennie Mackintosh and his Glasgow colleagues, to the German artistic public and, in turn, through his books

Above: Decorated cover of an early volume of *The Studio*, about 1900.

Left: Martin Battersby's Sussex Square flat in the late 1960s. The furnishings include a mirror-glass commode by Robert Block, a Legras glass vase and an Art Deco wrought-iron mirror-frame. The gouache design is by Erté, and sphinxes are ubiquitous.

and journals gave an identity to the work of *avant-garde* German and Austrian artists. He published *Deutsche Kunst und Dekoration*, *Die Kunst*, *Innen Dekoration* and *Das Interieur*. The other key figure, Julius Meier-Graefe, was an entrepreneur who had brought together a number of talented designers, not least the Belgian architect Henry Van de Velde, in the context of his Paris shop, La Maison Moderne, opened in 1898. He established a base in Munich where he published *Dekorative Kunst* and *Kunst und Handwerk*.

The wealth of German language journals in the period 1900–10 reflects the fecundity of Austrian and German artists at this time, a point noted by Battersby who shrewdly traces the Austro-German roots of Art Deco. He charts Paul Poiret's travels to Austria and Germany in 1909 where his observations of the Wiener Werkstätte inspired his own Atelier Martine; he notes the positive impression made by the unity of concept of the Munich Werkbund exhibit at the Salon d'Automne in 1910 and identifies influential motifs first published in the magazine *Die Kunst.*

In France, *Art et Décoration*, published from 1897, and *L'Art Décoratif*, from 1899, led the field. In the twenties and thirties *Mobilier et Décoration* and *L'Amour de l'Art*, both first published in 1921, gave an excellent coverage of both avant-garde and mainstream contemporary work. Through these decades the prevalent monopoly of monochrome illustration in art journals saw a notable exception in the high quality, complex, often multi-technique production of the magazine *L'Illustration*, which published regular colour features on the contemporary decorative arts. Battersby's library included special issues on the "Exposition des Arts Décoratifs" (25 April 1925), "Arts Décoratifs Modernes" (19 September 1925) and "Intérieurs Modernes" (27 May 1933), the latter illustrating schemes by Emile-Jacques Ruhlmann, Edgar Brandt, Eugène Printz, Jules Leleu, DIM and Paul

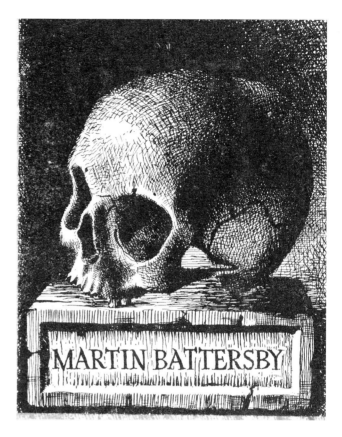

Above and left: Two book plates designed by Martin Battersby for himself.

Ruaud, and the special issue on the Paris 1937 Exhibition (14 August 1937).

The rise of these art periodicals was paralleled by the increasing popularity of fashion magazines in which halftone reproductions of photographs were gradually tipping the balance against line drawings. Condé Nast's *Vogue* and William Randolph Hearst's *Harper's Bazaar* established what has proved to be a longterm pre-eminence, as did, in its own particular field, Condé Nast's *House and Garden*, quoted by Battersby in both *The Decorative Twenties* and *The Decorative Thirties*. Battersby preserved a collection of *Vogue* and *Harper's Bazaar* covers by leading illustrators, notably Benito, Cassandre, Domergue, Erté, Laurencin and Lepape, a generation of artists whose work evidently touched his sensibilities far more than did that of the photographers who gradually usurped

their role. It is no coincidence that all these illustrators worked in France, for it is a matter of record, which Battersby systematically emphasized, that in the years immediately before and after the First World War the French established a supremacy in the decorative arts which they were to maintain, virtually unchallenged, until the Second World War.

Below: Charles Moreau's Librairie d'Art Industriel, 8 rue de Prague, Paris, designed by Romanet in about 1925: there are Art Deco references in the formalized flowers and leaves and the scrolled metalwork above the door.

This supremacy is underlined by the primacy of French publishing in the fields of fashion and the decorative arts. In the twenties, as Battersby details in *The Decorative Twenties*, books themselves became a focus of creative attention within a remarkable renaissance of the arts of illustrated book production and bookbinding. In the sphere of fashion, Battersby draws particular attention to the role of Lucien Vogel, a publisher of luxurious periodicals. Vogel is best remembered for his *Gazette du Bon Ton*, published from 1912 until 1925 when it was absorbed into *Vogue*, and his *Feuillets d'Art*, first published in 1919. Both set new standards of colour printing, using the *pochoir*, or

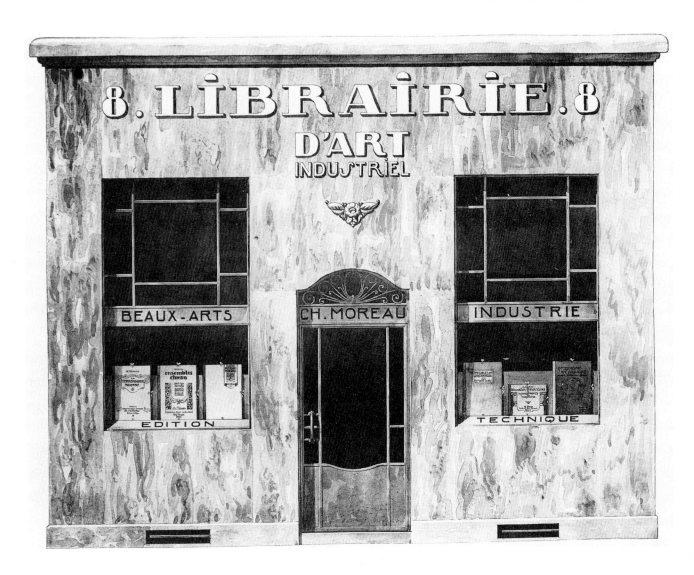

stencil colouring, process which created fashion plates of remarkable vibrancy. The *Gazette* was devoted to fashion, the *Feuillets* to fashion and art, with features on both historical and highly contemporary topics. It was the *Feuillets d'Art* which published the first article in France on Eileen Gray (noted in *The Decorative Twenties*). Battersby had runs of both journals on his shelves.

The French were systematic in documenting the emergence and flowering of their decorative arts in the aftermath of the First World War and there is a nationalistic bravura in a sequence of books tracing the genesis of Art Deco which were crucial to Battersby's researches. These included, most notably, works by Emile-Bayard, including *Le Style Moderne*, from the early twenties, and *L'Art Appliqué d'Aujourd'hui* of around 1925, and Gaston Quénioux's *Les Arts Décoratifs Modernes (France)*, 1925. To these should be added the twelve-volume record of the Paris 1925 Exhibition, entitled *Arts Décoratifs et Industriels Modernes*, published in 1925 by the Office Central d'Editions et de Librairies, and also in Battersby's library.

In documenting the decorative arts, perhaps the most notable publishing endeavour in France during the twenties and thirties was the issue of numerous finely produced folios on specific categories of creative activity. The leading publishers in this field were Charles Moreau, Albert Levy and Charles Massin. The folios, finely printed in photogravure, usually monochrome, occasionally with *pochoir* or colour separation plates, cover every category of the decorative arts and are a comprehensive record of French achievement.

Battersby's library included *La Ferronerie Moderne*, *La Sculpture Décorative Moderne*, and *Le Luminaire* published by Charles Moreau; *Etoffes d'Ameublement*, *Intérieurs en Couleurs–France* and *L'Art Décoratif Français 1918–1925* published by Albert Levy, who was, at this date, also publisher of *Art et Décora-*

Left: Boutique at the Salon des Artistes-Décorateurs designed by Kodjak for Charles Moreau in 1927: its clean, austere style marks the impact of Modernism.

Right: "Des Rubans", a *pochoir* plate by Georges Lepape from the *Gazette du Bon Ton*, published by Lucien Vogel.

tion; *Suggestions pour Etoffes et Tapis*, by E. A. Séguy, *Le Décor Moderne dans la Teinture et le Tissu*, and *Le Style Moderne dans la Décoration Intérieure*, published by Charles Massin.

Of particular note among the numerous other folios published are the record of interiors at the Paris 1925 Exhibition, *Ensembles Mobiliers—Exposition Internationale 1925*, compiled by Maurice Dufrène, published by Charles Moreau, and the series of twenty folios which constituted *L'Art International d'Aujourd'hui*, published around 1930 by Charles Moreau.

The general weakness of British or American as compared with French achievements is reflected in the relative paucity of available documentation. The contemporary reference works that were published are rarely of the quality of production that was the norm for their French counterparts. Battersby draws upon the writings of a host of prominent authors concerned with the applied arts, including Noel Carrington, Henry Dowling, Paul T. Frankl, John Gloag, Geoffrey Holme, Derek Patmore, Herbert Read and Shirley Wainwright. Even their collective impact, however, fails to dent the armour of French virtuosity.

The international aspects of Battersby's researches were greatly enriched by the many biographies, autobiographies, memoirs and, indeed, key works of contemporary fiction on his shelves. Such sources gave highly personal insights and anecdotal clues to the period or, in the case of the fictional works, highly evocative passages from which Battersby was able to draw in his concern to convey the flavour of the period. These sources included books by leading decorators, designers, artists and editors, among them Paul Poiret's *My First Fifty Years* (1931), Elsie de Wolfe's *After All* (1935), *Antoine* by Antoine (1945), Harold Acton's *Memoirs of an Aesthete* (1948), Edna Woolman Chase and Ilka Chase's *Always in Vogue* (1954), Schiaparelli's *Shocking Life* (1954), and Man Ray's *Self Portrait* (1963); novels which Battersby quoted include Edward James's Surrealistic *The Gardener Who Saw God* (1937), Nancy Mitford's *The Pursuit of Love* (1945) and Michael Arlen's *A Young Man Comes to London* (1932).

After the Second World War and with the excep-

tion of oblique references in occasional such memoirs, the cycle of fashion imposed an inevitable period of neglect on the decorative arts of the preceding decades. This period of rejection involved an automatic moratorium on research and publishing. Not until the mid sixties was the wheel of fashion to turn full circle and were the styles of the twenties and thirties to attract the attentions of a new generation.

The publications which reflect the beginnings of this revival include works of varying degrees of merit. In 1966, on the occasion of a major exhibition at the Musée des Arts Décoratifs, Paris, curator Yvonne Brunhammer edited the catalogue *Les Années '25: Art Deco/Bauhaus/Stijl/Esprit Nouveau*, and in the same year published *Lo Stile 1925*, an Italian-language work translated into English as *The Nineteen Twenties Style* (1969). Brunhammer's serious approach established her as a respected authority, a deserved reputation consolidated by her role as curator, author and editor of the two-part catalogue, *1925*, published in 1976 on the occasion of the belated fiftieth anniversary celebration of the Paris 1925 Exhibition.

Giulia Veronesi's *Stile 1925* (1966) translated into English under the title *Into the Twenties—Style and Design 1909–1929* (1968) was a rich and well considered survey. Madge Garland's *The Indecisive Decade* (1968) was a fascinating and remarkably comprehensive potpourri of recollections of the thirties. Bevis Hillier rode the crest of a fashionable wave with his amusing, journalistic forays *Art Deco* (1968) and *The World of Art Deco* (1971), though these two works may have encouraged a popular misunderstanding of the label Art Deco. Hillier used the title "Art Deco" to describe the full spectrum, and therefore, inevitably, the most widely disparate aspects of design and decorative art in the twenties and thirties. Battersby, Brunhammer and others since have applied the Art Deco label more narrowly and more judiciously, to describe a peculiarly French manifestation in the decorative arts which had its roots in the years before the First World War and found its apogee at the 1925 Exhibition.

Published respectively in 1969 and 1971, Martin Battersby's *The Decorative Twenties* and *The Decorative Thirties* attracted considerable and well deserved acclaim for their scope, their wealth of detail, observation and illustration, and for the convincing way in which their author evoked the atmosphere of these periods. Battersby's texts bore the stamp of his long-term interest in and often first-hand familiarity with his subject matter. The books reflect also the part played in the formation of his expertise by his in-depth knowledge of contemporary source books. Close study of these sources gave Battersby a firm framework within which to develop his own sharply defined ideas and observations and gave structure to his practical visual note-taking. The timing of the publication of Battersby's twin volumes was perfect. The books were widely enjoyed and provided a richly textured stimulus to a generation eager to learn about the styles of the twenties and thirties.

They were followed through the seventies and eighties by a constant flow of publications, sometimes more profusely illustrated, sometimes more specialized in subject, but rarely, if ever, written from such a deep understanding of the periods under discussion. There appeared luxuriously produced coffee-table books, both general and specific in subject matter,

exhibition catalogues and monographs. With a few notable exceptions, however, such as the Hayward Gallery, London, exhibition catalogue, *Thirties* (1980), or the Musée des Arts Décoratifs 1976 publication referred to above, the trend was towards publications which concentrated on artefacts in isolation from their social, historical or human context. Good examples of this genre were such works as Victor Arwas's *Art Deco Sculpture* (1975), *Glass—Art Nouveau to Art Deco* (1977) and *Art Deco* (1980); Pierre Kjellberg's *Art Deco—Les Maîtres du Mobilier* (1981) or the series of richly illustrated works published by José Alvarez in Paris under his imprint Les Editions du Regard. These include *Ruhlmann* (1983), *Chareau* (1984), *Printz* (1986) and *U.A.M.* (1986).

Too long out of print, Battersby's books make a timely reappearance and redress the balance of available documentation with their rich contextualizing of the decorative arts of the twenties and thirties.

PHILIPPE GARNER
November 1987

A sphinx motif designed by Battersby and used in
1964 in the catalogue to his show of sphinx
paintings at the Arthur Jeffress Gallery.

INTRODUCTION

To write a book about the twenties is an objective experience. When a period is sufficiently removed in time to place it in the area of history with most of its creative protagonists vanished, in some cases even from memory, the distinctive feel or atmosphere has to be reconstructed by patient research and a piecing together of fragments of information gleaned from the books and magazines of the period. The thirties is another matter. My direct involvement in the decorative arts in the 1930s, both as a member of the studio of one of the leading firms of decorators in London and later freelance as a mural painter and theatre designer, has both advantages and disadvantages. It is not possible to be entirely unbiased but at the same time actual experience of the conditions of the period gives a viewpoint which can shed a revealing light.

The thirties were far from being an ideal time to start a career in the decorative arts—if there has ever been such a time. Opportunities were limited, recognition difficult to achieve and the rewards less than meagre. For the young hoping for careers in architecture, painting or any branch of the decorative arts the prospects were bleak, with preference inevitably going to older and more experienced exponents with established reputations; the fact of being young was considered a disadvantage. Even an older genera-

tion with a record of solid achievement reaching back perhaps to the days before the Great War found it hard to make ends meet in the drab years of the Depression, and anyone fortunate enough to be in safe and congenial employment took care to hold on to his position at any cost. Few if any painters, for instance, could earn enough by the sale of their works alone and many an artist who has since become well known was glad, in the thirties, to paint decorative flower pieces or screens for interior decorators at say ten pounds a time or to design ceramics or textiles if the opportunity occurred.

Aesthetic theories played little part in practical creative life during the thirties, as anyone with actual experience of that period will testify. Herbert Read, John Gloag, John de la Vallette and others in England preached the gospel of fitness for purpose in books, lectures, articles and even broadcast talks, but their efforts met with indifference on the part of a buying public which resented being either instructed or patronized concerning the artefacts they were able to spare the money to purchase. Manufacturers were equally loath to add to their overheads by engaging outside designers with little experience of the required techniques—an understandable reaction when factories were closing down and banks were refusing to lend the money to finance new ventures. When the majority of manufacturers were learning to live with the idea of bankruptcy they had neither the means nor the inclination to further any revolutionary theories about design. The position of even established firms of in-

Left: Evening dress and fur cape by Lucien Lelong, early 1930s.

Left: The Pavillon de l'Esprit Nouveau, designed by Le Corbusier and his brother Pierre Jeanneret and shown at the Paris 1925 Exhibition. The sculpture in the foreground is by Lipchitz.

Right: The dining room of Erwin Piscator's apartment in Berlin, designed by Marcel Breuer of the Bauhaus in 1927.

terior decorators was precarious, threatened as they were by an increasing number of freelance competitors. In this field in particular the client was all-important and what the client wanted, the decorator had to provide. Even if the Bauhaus, by some turn of fate, had managed to survive throughout the thirties, it is extremely doubtful that its theories would have had more than a local influence and the decorative arts in England, France and the United States would probably have pursued their own course unaffected. As it was, few in England were aware of its existence—the spate of books and exhibitions concerned with the work of the Bauhaus since the mid sixties has probably made more people aware of its work and aims than at the time of its existence. Any interior decorator rash enough to try to persuade a client to embody its precepts in a decorative scheme would have met with short shrift—that is, assuming the highly unlikely fact that the decorator himself had heard of the Bauhaus. The excessive and frequently boring simplicity of many interior schemes of the early thirties was often a case of making a virtue out of a necessity—rooms were sparsely furnished because many people, young married couples, for instance, simply could not afford to

fill them with unnecessary furniture and accessories, however decorative. Then there were those, of course, who found this trend towards simplicity (advocated by so many contributors to *The Architectural Review* and similar periodicals) very much to their taste, whatever their income. Simultaneously, however, there was an even greater number of people who found bare rooms devoid of decorative objects unsympathetic and preferred to cover every available flat surface with ornaments—if not perhaps quite to the degree fashionable in the twenties or earlier periods. And it was this second trend which became increasingly prevalent as the decade advanced.

Inevitably any survey of the thirties must contain constant references to the Depression and to the state of political uncertainty which preoccupied the minds of many. But at the same time, despite these clouds, the thirties were a period of creative activity which is only now beginning to receive its just appreciation; in retrospect, it was a time when more originality and freedom of expression was permissible than is generally realized. It is to be hoped that this volume, though written from a personal point of view and experience, will help to eliminate many of the misconceptions which have arisen about a decade which tends to be overshadowed by the more spectacular achievements of the twenties.

"It's rather sad", she said one day, "to belong, as we do, to a lost generation. I'm sure in history the two wars will count as one war and that we shall be squashed out of it altogether, and people will forget that we ever existed. We might just as well have never lived at all, I do think it's a shame."

"It may become a sort of literary curiosity," Davey said. "People will be interested in it for all the wrong reasons, and collect Lalique dressing-table sets and shagreen boxes and cocktail cabinets lined with looking-glass and find them very amusing."

(Nancy Mitford, *The Pursuit of Love*, London, 1945.)

I
THE BACKGROUND

T he thirties were born prematurely and disastrously on Thursday 24 October 1929 when the New York Stock Exchange closed its doors. The events of that day were to affect the lives of millions, directly or indirectly, for years to come. The previous decade, for all its reputation of hectic gaiety, had had its realities of disillusion and hardship and to many the Depression of the early thirties spelt out the end of any hopes they may have had. For others—and they were in the majority—the bright bubble of a false prosperity vanished overnight, leaving them in a seemingly endless twilight of poverty and hopelessness. The arts survived as they always do, for there were still a number of rich patrons who were either unaffected by the recurring financial crises or even richer as a result of those same crises.

It is the aim of this volume to trace the progress of the decorative arts through the thirties, a progress leading from the austerities of the early years of the decade to the more prosperous times before the Second World War when for a brief period romanticism and fantasy were triumphant.

Left: The main room of a house designed by Professor Adolf Rading in 1932: his brief had been to build, on a strictly limited budget, a modest, unostentatious house, incorporating "spiritual values", using just space and colour to provide decoration. The room was olive green, with red doors and a linoleum floor of large squares in white, blue, red, grey and black. The decorative metal construction on the wall was a "space-enlivening element" by Oskar Schlemmer.

In the years following the First World War the trend of taste in the decorative arts was dictated by the artists and designers active before 1914. On the cessation of hostilities the natural thing for them was to continue where they had left off—a return to the conditions prevailing before the war. Money was plentiful with the emergence of a new class of war profiteers anxious to enjoy their new wealth, and for a considerable period the problem for the luxury trades was not a shortage of clients so much as a need for skilled craftsmen and materials. In some trades a new generation of workers had to be trained; in France hundreds of factories in the battle areas had been destroyed. The luxury fabrics, for instance, upon which France depended for her supremacy in fashion, were in short supply. The lack of well-seasoned timber for fine furniture was general. Trade and export, particularly to the United States, were of prime importance to countries faced with colossal war debts. A return to something approaching normality was essential.

In each country the problem of catering for the prevailing taste was different. In France the devotion to the furniture and decoration of the eighteenth and to a lesser extent the early nineteenth centuries was as strong as ever, tempered with that desire for novelty which led the Parisians to be compared with the Athenians of classical times. The brief reign of Art Nouveau from the mid 1890s to the early 1900s, a period of little more than ten years, produced a sharp reaction even among its most enthusiastic supporters and came to be regarded with as much disdain in France as it had generally been in England. This essentially linear style, lyrically described by Raymond Cogniat as "irises, water lilies and convolvulus—precious flowers languorously decomposing in tender harmonies", was succeeded after a brief hiatus by another style equally linear in which the sinuous curves of Art Nouveau were controlled into circles and ovals, the naturalistic flowers formalized into geometric patterns and the delicate nuances replaced by vivid tones of cerise, orange, violet, emerald and lapis. This style, referred to as Art Deco as early as 1935, has since become generally known by this name, an abbreviation of the title of the Exposition Internationale des Arts Décoratifs et Industriels Modernes held in Paris in 1925, an exhibition so successful that in the ensuing years it came to be used as a standard of comparison for subsequent exhibitions.

The sources of the style were various. Its vibrant colouring came from the Russian Ballet and the designs of Léon Bakst, in particular his setting and costumes for *Scheherazade* when it opened in Paris in 1910. The leading couturier Paul Poiret was producing a wealth of fantastic, sometimes bizarre, designs in a similar vein. The decorative motifs owed more than a little to the Austrian designers Dagobert Peche and Josef Hoffmann. Interest in their work had come about as a result of the 1910 Exhibition of Applied Art from Munich which had earned the disapproval of Parisian critics but had nevertheless been sufficiently popular for mounted police to be brought in to control the crowds waiting for admission. Hoffman, in particular, among the many designers in Germany and Austria, was influenced to a considerable extent by the work of Charles Rennie Mackintosh. Fifteen years before, his work had been ignored in France where artists and designers had been preoccupied with their own elegant and sophisticated variations on Art Nouveau themes. After a period of time, however, and when the decorative imagery of Mackintosh had been transmuted through Germany and Austrian sources, Parisians were captivated.

The sometimes wayward and perverse outlines of Art Nouveau furniture were replaced by a more controlled style which had its origins in the Directoire and Consulate styles created during the revolutionary period (and in essentials simplified versions of Louis XVI), with a suggestion of the more ponderous Empire period which followed. Equally, the fashions of the years around 1910 as depicted by Paul Iribe and George Barbier show the Directoire influence in their long straight lines combined with applied ornaments of oriental motifs. After the Armistice the designers of both dress and interiors resumed where they had left off five years before. Many architects and decorating concerns were still preparing for the exhibition which originally had been planned for 1915, had been postponed owing to the war and after several delays finally took place in 1925.

Two of the leading figures during the period that Art Deco was at its height were Paul Poiret and Jeanne Lanvin. Poiret has often been erroneously described as being the arbiter of taste before the First World War with a decline in power during the twenties, but in fact his influence was even stronger during most of the twenties, as a result of the decors and fabrics designed in his Atelier Martine, and his period of decline dates from the very end of the decade, when his financial problems became serious. During the twenties his *salon de couture* was a meeting place for rich, elegant women with aspirations to be regarded as leaders of fashion, his passion for collecting paintings brought him into contact with new and promising artists, while the perpetual need for new ideas and inspiration brought most of the young designers into his orbit at one time or another.

Jeanne Lanvin was in a similar position as a leader of taste—celebrated as a couturière and a decorator though not to the same extent as Poiret. Besides these two there were a number of designers supervising the decorating departments of the big Parisian department stores—Paul Follot, whose work in the Art Nouveau style had been featured at La Maison Moderne at the turn of the century and who was now designing in the Art Deco manner for the Atelier Pomone at Bon Marché; Maurice Dufrène, similarly adapting to a new idiom as the head of La Maîtrise at the Galeries Lafayette; Louis Sognot at Printemps and Etienne Kohlmann at the Magasins du Louvre. Eugène Süe and André Mare, like André

Groult, were creating interiors and furniture based on the forms of the late eighteenth century while Emile-Jacques Ruhlmann, a dominant figure during the twenties, became more and more inclined to follow the traditions of the heavier and more sombre Empire style.

Considerable misunderstanding has arisen as to the exact use of the terms "Art Deco and "Modernist" and the two names are often incorrectly applied. At its best the effect of Art Deco was one of elegant luxury, of a delight in ornament for its own sake, while the rather restricted range of decorative motifs gave an overall unity of style, which made it applicable to anything from the façade of a building to the decoration of a vanity case, and an immediately recognizable character. In the 1925 Exhibition Art Deco was seen at its most luxuriant.

This exhibition was however at once the apogee and the finale of Art Deco. A curious parallel with Art Nouveau can be found, for this style too was seen at its best in the exhibits for the 1900 Exhibition and suffered, with a few exceptions, a sharp decline in public favour very soon after. Possibly the artists and designers working in each style—and there were a number who adapted from one to the other and whose work appeared in both exhibitions—experienced a revulsion of feeling on seeing the particular decorative idiom which they had helped to create commercialized and cheapened by unintelligent plagiarism. The changing and often illogical movement of fashion will have played its part. In the case of Art Deco, which had been flourishing since before the Great War, a change was overdue, especially in the rapidly moving times of the postwar period. Like Art Nouveau it was a fashion directed almost exclusively towards women, applied to the rooms they used and the objects which surrounded them. But in the early twenties women were beginning to rebel against the role imposed upon them and were no longer content to remain passive decorative objects extravagantly dressed and hatted and posing like odalisques in exotic surroundings reminiscent of the *Arabian Nights*. The shortage of manpower which resulted from the war gave many women opportunities for more active and useful lives. The pursuit of a career in business or even in sport

became possible to women. The new feeling was for freedom and simplicity combined with a somewhat hectic gaiety symbolized by the prevailing rhythms of jazz and this new feeling found expression in the angularities of Modernism.

Even before 1925 there had been signs of a reaction against the sensuous curves of Art Deco. The creative ferment which first manifested itself about 1905 in Cubism and its elaborations of analytical, synthetic and orphic Cubism and an allied interest in African tribal art, was reinforced by the post-war development of Purism, a movement exemplified by *Après le Cubisme* published in 1918 by Ozenfant and Le Corbusier. The authors accused the followers of

Cover of an early issue of *De Stijl*, 1920.

Woodcut illustration by Lyonel Feininger for Walter Gropius's Bauhaus Manifesto, 1919.

tion of these two artists in the ballet *La Chatte* with its decor of transparent talc and black American oilcloth was instrumental in bringing Constructivism to a wider audience, and demonstrated the desire of Serge Diaghilev to break away from the exoticism of the earlier ballets such as *Scheherazade*, *Thamar* or *Le Dieu Bleu*. A similar rejection of ornament and an insistence on elementary colours and linear abstraction were the tenets of those following De Stijl, a Dutch movement originally founded by Theo van Doesburg and named after the magazine launched by him in 1917.

The most notable of these movements was that developed at the Bauhaus founded in 1919 by Walter Gropius at Weimar and after 1925 situated in Dessau. The teachings covered all branches of art from architecture to typography, with the aim of amalgamating the best of craftwork with the needs of industry. Among its teachers were Paul Klee, Oskar Schlemmer, Laszlo Moholy-Nagy and Ludwig Mies van der Rohe. But these revolutionary ideas current in Holland, Germany and Russia were for the most part ignored in Paris and London during the twenties.

FRANCE

France has always been the home of the *avant-garde* —within limits. As an acknowledged leader of fashion Paris has always had a reputation for luxurious elegance and the country's economic balance has depended largely on the maintenance of this reputation, which has always, and particularly in the twenties and thirties, attracted the rich and discriminating from many other countries. Their patronage meant the livelihood of a vast number of artists, designers and craftsmen whose aim was to divert and astonish with masterpieces of invention and skill.

The ideas of mass production and of designing simple, handsome objects which could be produced in indefinite quantities by machinery, with a consequent loss of individuality—ideas which lay behind most of the theories advanced by the Bauhaus, for instance —would have been abhorrent to any French person priding himself on his taste during the twenties and thirties. In addition, the mere fact that these ideas

Cubism of allowing it to degenerate into decoration, and advocated an impersonal art stripped of ornament and even individuality, owing its inspiration to the machine. The Russian concept of Constructivism propagated by Vladimir Tatlin, Naum Gabo and Anton Pevsner, with its insistence on abstraction and the use of new materials such as perspex, had a considerable influence on architecture, theatre design and sculpture and its ideals were taken to Paris in 1921 by Pevsner and to Germany by Gabo. The collabora-

emanated from countries whose reputation for taste had never been highly regarded in France was enough to put them out of court. It was only when these concepts were filtered through the work of *avant-garde* French designers that they became acceptable to French patrons. Ernest Tisserand writing in *L'Amour de l'Art* in 1929 on the controversial question of steel furniture implies that the first tubular steel chair was a French creation and nowhere in his article mentions the name of Marcel Breuer, who was actually responsible for the first such chair in 1925.

The older generation of designers in Paris were too established to change their conceptions of design easily. Some had already experienced their own revolt against Art Nouveau a quarter of a century before and could not adapt to yet another style and, in addition, they had a faithful clientele who could see no virtues in Modernism. The critic Guillaume Janneau did not

conceal his scepticism about the importance of contemporary German trends. Reviewing the exhibits at the autumn Salon des Artistes-Décorateurs in 1930 and, in particular, the specially invited German section, he commends Gropius and Breuer as "daring moderns, informed and courageous in the expression of their ideas", but continues: "French artists have revealed themselves as very impressed by the strength of impulse they feel to be behind this section. If they had ever visited Germany, the new Germany that has arisen during the ten years since the war, they would discover a complete native absence of this formula. In actuality, it is something of a hot-house plant. It would be just as false to judge the activities of modern Germany by the theories of this numerically ill-equipped vanguard as to judge our own by the opinions of a few of our already outmoded theorists. In fact, before two years were out, wearied of this application and the ineradicable monotony of effect it must produce, we would joyfully return to little porcelain flowers and mother-of-pearl inlays." Janneau's words were prophetic.

It was the younger generation of architects and

Chaise longue by René Herbst, part of the furnishings of the palace of the Maharajah of Indore, decorated in the Modernist style in 1930–33.

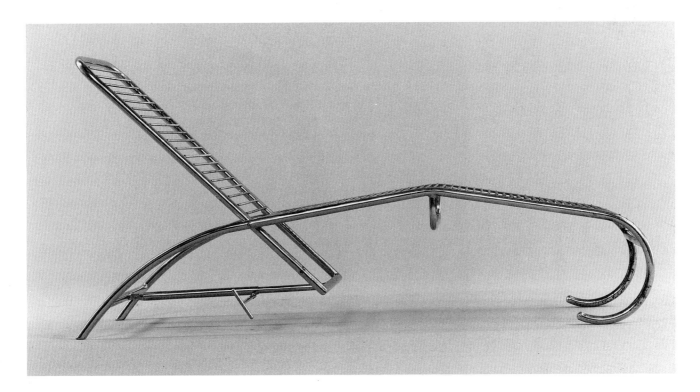

COIFFEUR GIRAULT PARFUMEUR

COIFFEUR POUR MESSIEURS

designers, including Robert Mallet Stevens, Eugène Printz, Pierre Chareau, Francis Jourdain, René Herbst, Charlotte Perriand, Le Corbusier and his cousin Pierre Jeanneret, who were able, against considerable hostility, to impose their ideas, but after a first enthusiasm for the austerities of steel, glass and bare walls, even these designers found their clients inclined to temper the clinical atmosphere with fur, velvet and lacquer.

The best method of showing the difference be-

Left: The Art Deco façade of Girault, Boulevard des Capucines, Paris, designed by the architectural firm of Azema, Edrei et Hardy in the early 1920s.

Below: The Modernist façade of Covanna, rue Pasquier, Paris, designed by Pierre Patout in 1927.

tween Art Deco and Modernism is by comparing an Art Deco shop front, for instance, with one designed in the Modernist manner. Azema, Edrei and Hardy's design for the façade of the hairdressing establishment Girault in the Boulevard des Capucines employs practically every motif in the Art Deco repertoire. The lavish use of wrought ironwork contrasts with stone, the metal with its profusion of conventionalized flowers being treated almost as a lace curtain. Closer examination reveals the use of the spiral (a form natural to the techniques of wrought iron), either as a termination of a graceful curve or as a repeated motif. The metal flowers include the characteristic formalizations of roses, sunflowers, dahlias and zinnias set upon smoothly sinuous stems to create an effect of

elegance and luxury. The octagonal panel which appears time and time again in Art Deco designs is here found in the centre window of the mezzanine floor and the only motif which is not incorporated is that of the elongated oval. The lettering of hammered iron, although not altogether happy in design, is gracefully appropriate, while the two female heads in relief on the pilaster and the mysterious half-mask over the entrance door are reminders that this is the façade of a temple of femininity—despite the announcement "Coiffeur pour Messieurs" and the masculine toiletries displayed in one window.

This shop front, dating probably from the early twenties, is in complete contrast with that of Covanna,

designed by Patout in 1927. Curves have been banished in favour of a rigidly balanced geometric arrangement of shapes and, except for the cross-hammered frames of the three upper windows and geometrical ventilation panels under the two ground-floor windows, the intricate ironwork has disappeared too. The fundamental simplicity of the design is made more interesting by the shadows caused by the projection and recession of the various elements such as the deep cornice and the raised lettering. The broad band of coloured geometrical ornament—possibly made more obtrusive by the effects of photography—is reminiscent of the *simultané* designs of Sonia Delaunay.

ENGLAND

In England there was a deep attachment to historicism, for the inclination was to regard taste as having ended somewhere around 1780 and new houses both large and small, together with their interior decorations, were conceived in the styles of the sixteenth, seventeenth and eighteenth centuries. A Tudor cottage, sham if the real thing were not available, was considered to be the ideal home in the country and if it were half-timbered and with a thatched roof so much the better, especially if furnished with more or less "Tudor" antiques. Alternatively, Georgian or Neo-Georgian houses were permissible as being rather more convenient and comfortable, and having the advantage that furniture in the Chinese taste could be incorporated in the decorative schemes to lend an air of genteel exoticism.

When materials and labour became available vast quantities of furniture were made in the Tudor, Queen Anne and Chippendale or Sheraton styles and although most of these pieces were obvious pastiches,

The historicist style in decoration is shown clearly in the reception room in Anthony Prinsep's house, 1935 (*left*), and the dining room in Frank Salisbury's manor house in 1933, with furniture in the popular neo-Elizabethan style (*below*).

enough of considerable quality and accuracy of period detail emerged to double—at the most moderate estimate—the number of "antiques" on the market in the following decades. The description "modern" of a piece meant only one thing—it was a contemporary reproduction of an antique. The nearest approach to a contemporary idiom in furniture design was in the worthy but, it must be said, somewhat dull, beautifully hand-made pieces in the style of the Arts and Crafts movement (then still in existence but losing ground as a decisive influence) and even these had strong traditional features. The attitude of looking back at the past was fostered by the large firms of decorators who had a virtual monopoly of such interior decoration as was not considered the province of the architect. The individual decorator exploiting his own personal taste and knowledge and working in a close consultation with the client was almost unknown. Those with an individual taste and able to plan original and striking backgrounds for their lives needed neither architect nor decorator. In the main, however, the advice of the salesmen in the large decorating establishments was sought, whether for the entire redecoration of a house or the choice of a piece of fabric for a cushion, and as most of these firms carried a large stock of antique or reproduction furniture together with fabrics reproducing old patterns, the client was induced as a matter of course to perpetuate the cult of historicism.

The designer Paul Nash in *Room and Book* has a number of caustic comments to make concerning this nostalgia for the past: "There exists in the English character an extraordinary sentiment, which baldly stated is that everything new is ugly and everything old is beautiful"; elsewhere he remarks, "the craze for the antique is bred in snobbery and survives in lazy-mindedness or is imposed on the ignorant and credulous by ignorant tradesmen." *Room and Book* was published in 1932 when efforts had already been made to improve the taste of the general public, and the gospel of design through fitness for purpose had been put forward by a number of architects and designers. So far their efforts had met with little success in weaning the public taste away from the olde worlde and Nash comments: "It must be admitted that at the present time in 1932 the taste for the antique is the favourite flavour of eighty per cent of the population or at least is supposed to be by the builder and furniture makers . . . there have been certain cross currents persistently flowing, by far the strongest of which is the Lethe-like stream of the Antique. These waters of forgetfulness roll down their preposterous logs of old oak, rosewood, and mahogany to some undefined limbo of dead things where no doubt a herd of white elephants will carry them wherever they are going. For antique furniture is the possession and often the product of people who wish to forget they are living today, the symbol of a sentimental nostalgia fostered by dealers in ghosts." In his view the English taste could be summed up as a "gabled house with bogus beams and lattice windows, a sham inglenook and a gas log fire; Old English chintz and Persian carpets . . . a teacosy of Jacobean design . . . an endless dance of ancient masks like a fearful fancy dress ball composed of nothing but travesties of the Jacobeans and poor Queen Anne."

An advertisement of 1930 for antique furniture, published by a London department store, incorporated in the caption a gem of unconscious humour. "Place on top of an Old English desk a gem of a Queen Anne mirror and you have a dressing table a queen or an American would envy"; and the fact that both table and mirror even in the photograph are obvious reproductions adds a further twist.

Herbert Read's championship of Walter Gropius and the ideals of the Bauhaus took the form of a lecture to the Design and Industries Association which was reprinted in the *Journal of the Royal Institute of British Architects* in May 1934, and his book *Art and Industry* was written "to support and propagate the ideals expressed by Dr Gropius", but the results were minimal in England. Apart from a few illustrated articles in *The Studio* and *The Architectural Review*, little notice was taken of the work of the pioneers on the Continent and a traditional attitude left no room for new concepts, except to a very limited extent in architecture. *The Architectural Review*, as its name implies, was published for the architectural profession: its editors, whenever possible, reported and illustrated the best contemporary work on the Continent, and as a result a number of English architects picked up the superficial elements and mannerisms of the more extreme European examples, which they super-imposed on traditional plans. The case is on record of a well-known firm of architects who had been commissioned to build a large country house in the Neo-Georgian style for a millionaire: just as the plans and elevations were finalized, their client visited an international exhibition and, taken by the modern architecture, decided to have his house built in the contemporary style instead. The architects simply eliminated all ornament and mouldings from the façades, substituted horizontal steel windows (to the later chagrin of the interior decorators) and had the brick surfaces covered in stucco. The theories of Le Corbusier, Gropius and other masters of modern architecture on the relationships of space, of the interior to the exterior, or of the suitability of the

building to its surroundings need never have been formulated.

"Where is your vorticist?" asked Wyndham Lewis in 1934. "A handful of modernist villas have been put up; a few big factories have gone cubist . . . one shop in a hundred has acquired a chromium-plated façade but only in the big cities."

The word "Modernistic" itself had its detractors, despite its practical value in indicating the difference between contemporary design and a pastiche of the antique. Paul Nash, while offering no alternative, described "Modernistic" as a "repellent title" and regarded commercial Modernism as the most formidable obstacle to the new movement, adding that "just as at an earlier date persons and things were referred to as 'so artistic', now they are described as 'quite modernistic' and in such case one knows only too well what to expect. The modernistic craze is kept lively by the same stimuli as the antique vogue—snobbery and delusion." Here Paul Nash in his writings reflects an attitude common among the advocates of what he describes as the "new movement"—the belief that

House in Church Street, Chelsea, London, designed by Maxwell Fry and Walter Gropius in the Modernist style.

because many people preferred to live surrounded by the artefacts of a past century they were at best snobs and at worst the mindless slaves of fashion. He and many others seemed unwilling to accept the fact that a love of the antique could be genuine.

THE UNITED STATES

American interior design changed in every aspect during the thirties. Commenting on the state of design in the United States in 1930 *The Studio* made the point that "the modern furniture movement is only a little more than four years old", although there had been a few courageous pioneers earlier, and in a review during the same year of an international exhibition of glass and rugs at the Metropolitan Museum of Art the opinion is given that "American exhibits cannot bear comparison with those from other countries", with the significant addition that France and Sweden, both prominent in these fields, had refused to cooperate for fear of plagiarism. The American designer Paul Frankl in *New Dimensions* published in 1930 explains that "the only reason why America was not represented at the exhibition of decorative industrial art held in Paris in 1925 was because we found that we had no decorative

Below left: An American dining room of the 1930s—neo-Regency furniture in a modern environment.

Right: A scaled-down sitting room, one of the miniature schemes presented by McMillen Inc., 1932.

art. Not only was there a sad lack of any achievement that could be exhibited, but we discovered that there was not even a serious movement in this direction and that the general public was quite unconscious of the fact that modern art had been extended into the field of business and industry. On the other hand, we had our skyscrapers, and at that very date they had been developed to such an extent that, if it had been possible to have sent an entire building abroad, it would have been a more vital contribution in the field of modern art than all the things done in Europe added together."

But by 1937 *The Studio* is recording that in America "professional designers of interiors not only influence fashion but control the purchases of two hundred thousand influential clients". No reference was given for this figure but it indicated that in a short space of time the profession of interior decorator had become very much a part of American life.

As in England and France there was—and still is—a certain number of wealthy patrons with a preference for the styles of the past and if all these people were not able to buy the antique furniture and paintings imported by Joseph Duveen or Elsie de Wolfe, they still preferred to live in surroundings reminiscent of the past epochs of England, France, Spain or Italy. It was solemnly announced in an American periodical that "Mr Charles Duveen, the international decorator, will continue to purvey his originals copied from Chippendale and Adam and all the famous eighteenth-century craftsmen: Macy will have copies of the copies." Modernism was not allowed in the house beyond the bathroom or the kitchen, and tastes were untouched by passing enthusiasms for "amusing" revivals of periods not regarded as classic. And at the same time as the more advanced designers were working in a Modernist idiom there were others who favoured an updated version of historic periods.

A modernized version of Regency and Empire styles characterized the majority of a series of miniature rooms designed and exhibited by McMillen, Inc. early in 1932. Constructed to the scale of one eighth, they were perfect replicas, even to the lighting fixtures, ornaments and a typewriter, of possible schemes of decoration for entrance halls, dining rooms, living rooms and bedrooms. A number of artists, including Jans Juta, the sculptor Boris Lovet-Lorski (who numbered Mary Pickford among his pupils) and Bernard Boutet de Monval, created miniature works of art, decorative features or replicas of portraits for the various rooms. In one living room the pared-down simplicity of the decorations, the three-quarter columns without capitals or bases and the limiting of decoration to bands of fluting suggest rather than reproduce a period style, at the same time

"Skyscraper" bookcase by Paul Frankl made in California redwood, late 1920s.

providing a harmonious background for the black and gold Regency furniture, reproduced in miniature with painstaking craftsmanship and probably replicas of actual pieces in stock at the time. A number of interiors in a similar style, a compromise between Modernism and Regency, appeared in periodicals in the early thirties, some of them showing an obvious debt to the designs of Sir John Soane, an architect much admired in Scandinavia.

But in spite of the Depression, or because of it, there was a growing taste for Modernism, a stream-lined expression of the American spirit in glittering chromium plate, mirror and tubular lighting—a realization of a new machine-made world of drive and efficiency, not uninfluenced by the movies and far removed from the harsh realities of economic strains, a reflection of the comparison, made in 1933, that "while English interiors are domestic and reticent, the French had an air of feminine luxury and the Germans stark and utilitarian, the American interior was different, had something exhilarating in its use of new forms and was occasionally theatrical." This may perhaps be attributed to the fact that a number of the leading designers in America, Lee Simonson, Norman Bel Geddes and Joseph Urban, for instance, were also simultaneously working as stage designers.

Modernism, with a growing emphasis on the machine as a source of inspiration for design and an often exaggerated stress on the dubious virtues of "streamlining", had in the late thirties brought about the emergence of a new figure—the industrial designer. His role became one of vital importance in the long years of the Depression when "styling" became one of the integral features in sales promotion. A newly styled object or piece of household equipment became something to be acquired as a status symbol and a proof that the owner was unaffected by the Depression—at least until the manufacturers produced a restyled model which made the previous one old-fashioned and obsolete. There must have been many English designers who read with astonished envy of the fees commanded by their opposite numbers as recorded in *Fortune* and quoted in an English periodical. Norman Bel Geddes was said to obtain a flat fee ranging from $1000 to $100,000 plus royalties

Radio in black painted wood and blue mirror-glass designed by
Walter Dorwin Teague, 1936.

for designing such items as a radio or a gas range;
Walter Dorwin Teague, the industrial, advertising and
interior designer, worked on a retainer of $12,000 to
$24,000 and Raymond Loewy could ask sums in a
similar range. The English equivalents of the corpor-
ations for which these and other designers worked
were, of course, with a limited market for their products, on a far smaller scale, but even taking this into
consideration the sums they expected to pay for new
designs were infinitesimal in comparison—even
when they considered a designer necessary.

America took to Modernism with an enthusiasm
unequalled in England. "Our age is one of invention,
machinery, industry, science and commerce . . . modern furniture has several strong characteristics. It is
built in flat surfaces and strong lines. The angles are

decided and sharp. The proportions are well considered and the finish is beyond reproach. Sentimental moulding and panelling are avoided as much as
possible in order to gain the effect of extreme and
severe simplicity," wrote Paul Frankl in 1930. The
description of a moulding as being "sentimental"
seems as curious to a present day viewpoint as the
comment of Frederick Everard, the head of the drawing office in a London firm, who wrote to *The Studio*
complaining that "modern furniture is finished in an
extremely effeminate and aesthetic tone . . . today we
are letting the atmosphere of the Continental Casino
invade our homes."

In many ways the Bauhaus ideals found their
fullest expression in the United States. Many of those
associated with the Bauhaus found refuge in America
after its closure by the Nazis in 1933 and their
teachings undoubtedly influenced the more *avant-
garde* design in that country to a greater extent than
anywhere else.

2

THE DEPRESSION AND ITS IMPACT ON THE DECORATIVE ARTS

T he Wall Street Crash of October 1929 brought about a world-wide depression which directly and indirectly affected the lives and fortunes of most people, whatever their occupation, until 1935. For about two years before there had been a wave of speculation in the United States, a gambling fever which manifested itself in an optimistic but ignorant investing in stocks and shares. The prices of shares rose or were driven up by unscrupulous operators to unparalleled levels until the inevitable time when shares were unloaded to take advantage of the prices and the market finally crashed. In twenty-four hours the value of shares fell to approximately their normal level and hundreds of thousands of speculators lost their investments. A rush upon capital in the banks proved too much for their resources and in the confusion a number of small banks closed their doors and in so doing placed the resources of the larger banking combines in jeopardy. In the following month it looked as though the downward movement had eased and a small amount of cautious buying of

shares started, but again the market broke, a pattern to be repeated in the following spring of 1930 and again six months later. By some mysterious process incomprehensible to laymen the financial experts maintained that in fact no real loss of wealth had occurred and that the gold reserves of the United States were actually greater than before, but these statements gave little consolation to the ruined investors and the millions of unemployed. The stories of bankrupted financiers throwing themselves in despair from the windows of their offices in skyscrapers, of the family of millionaires who embarked on a liner at New York *en route* to Paris and found themselves destitute on landing at Cherbourg, of Americans living in Paris who had to borrow money from their French servants, have become part of American folklore and, true or apocryphal, they illustrate the dramatic suddenness of the ruin which marked the end of the twenties.

England had suffered a financial setback on a far smaller scale in September 1929 when the collapse of the Clarence Hatry financial bubble had shaken the economic structure. The postwar boom in the United States had not been equalled in England and with less loose money for investment the English stock market was less affected by the fever of speculation raging

Left: Salon in the *Normandie* luxury suite ''Deauville'', decorated by Louis Süe.

across the Atlantic. But if the English were spared the immediate disaster they could not in the long run escape the results of that disaster.

The panic cancelling of all projects in America immediately hit the luxury trade and the art world. Art dealers in London and Paris who had enjoyed prosperous years exporting old masters found that their market in the United States had vanished overnight, with the additional blow that many of the works of art delivered were not yet paid for and were not likely to be paid for. Cartier's had so much jewelry in America that it was necessary to send a member of the firm to collect those pieces for which there was no possibility of payment. The many Americans who had led a carefree existence in Paris where, owing to a favourable rate of exchange, they could live on a far higher scale than in the States, hastily left for America and with them departed the market for paintings by hundreds of second-rate painters of the Ecole de Paris.

The efforts of French couturiers, hoteliers and shopkeepers to retain the American market were wryly described by Mieda Monro, an American resident in Paris and a contributor to *Town and Country*. She related how in 1932 all the dressmakers had slashed the prices of their models—Chanel halving her prices—while maintaining the standards of quality of fabric and workmanship, a drastic reduction which must have given some of the shrewder American patrons of the couturiers food for thought. Shops devoted to luxury goods in the rue Saint-Honoré broke the custom of closing on Monday and went further by reducing their prices on that day to compete with the big department stores which remained closed. Chanel and Schiaparelli designed evening dresses of cotton, a revolutionary step viewed with dismay by the silk manufacturers. One hotel was specially opened out of season for a single American family and the most celebrated restaurants advertised *prix-fixe* luncheons including unlimited wine.

Early in 1930 the Depression had had little effect as yet upon the English economy and it was not necessary to be rich to have an apartment in Paris as well as one in London. Rents were, if anything, lower in France than in England—a bachelor apartment in the Palais Royal could be had for £125 a year furnished,

and a ten-room apartment with a view over the Seine would entail an outlay of only £300 a year. Towards the end of 1930, however, only the richest English or Americans were able to maintain the luxury of a second home in Paris.

But France was probably less affected by the Depression than the United States or England. Though the luxury trades suffered from the sudden loss of the English and particularly the US market, there were still many rich clients from other countries, like India and South America. And even in the United States, after the first panic had subsided, there were people rich enough to order costly work in quantity. So, for example, although the demand for decorative lacquer panels and furniture—necessarily expensive through the skill and patience required in their making—should have been one of the first casualties, the lacquer worker Jean Dunand seems to have been unaffected by the general depression of the early thirties.

THE NORMANDIE

The policy of the French government to encourage any skill or craft in order to foster prestige helped many branches of the luxury trades to survive. Major sources of work for French craftsmen in the thirties were commissions for such symbols of national prestige as the luxury liner *Normandie*.

The *Normandie* was launched in 1932 and put into service with a maiden voyage in 1935. She was conceived and designed in terms of superlatives, for under the stipulations of the contract between the French line and the government the new vessel "had to be not less than equal to the best foreign ship in commission or under construction". This condition entailed the construction of a liner larger than any other afloat—a statistic much quoted to the press was that the length of the *Normandie* was greater than the height of the Eiffel Tower. And the boat had to exceed in luxury of decorations as much as it did in size the same line's *Ile de France* which had made its maiden trip in 1927. The *Normandie*'s gross tonnage was nearly twice as much as that of its predecessor and with this amount of space at their disposal the designers of the public rooms were enabled to achieve spectacular results. The author Ludwig Bemelmans was a passenger on the maiden voyage and his comment on the *Normandie* was that "she leaned to excesses in her decor—there was something of the fatal woman". The main dining room, 305 feet (93 metres) in length, 46 feet (14 metres) wide and 25 feet (7.5 metres) high, had walls sheathed in hammered glass panels and seven hundred passengers could dine by the light of thirty-eight wall panels, two gigantic chandeliers and twelve decorative standard lights, all the creation of René Lalique. Additional embellishments were four panels

The *Normandie* smoking room, with wall panels by Jean Dunand of lacquered and gilt gesso, carved in bas relief.

20 feet (6 metres) high of gilded plaster representing aspects of life in Normandy and a twice-life-size statue of "La Paix" in gilded bronze by Dejean. Off this vast room led eight private dining rooms each decorated with mural paintings by leading contemporary artists and an extra banqueting room with bas reliefs by Janniot.

The main lounge, slightly smaller than the dining room, contained four panels by Jean Dupas representing the history of navigation. Each panel, 50 feet (15.25 metres) wide and 22 feet (6.75 metres) in height was executed in a complicated technique which involved etching and painting the designs on the back of the glass, an arduous process which entailed working in reverse. The gilded furniture by Goudissart was covered in tapestry representing the flowers of the French colonies in tones of red, orange and grey; the

carpet by the same designer was claimed to be one of the largest ever woven in one piece and the windows were covered at night by embroidered silk curtains.

The transatlantic liners served the purpose, apart from transporting passengers quickly and comfortably, of providing a showcase for the work of the best designers of the country and the smoking room of the *Normandie* was devoted to the creations of Jean Dunand, long esteemed as one of the finest craftsmen in France. The walls were covered with panels, 22 feet (6.75 metres) high and 27 feet (8 metres) wide, of lacquer carved in relief after the style of Chinese coromandel screens, and depicted various activities treated in a quasi-oriental manner, one composition of life-size galloping horses being particularly handsome. To avoid damage to the precious lacquer by the movement of the ship, each panel was divided into smaller sections framed in copper. The small occasional tables and the frames of the brown morocco-covered chairs were also lacquered by Jean Dunand and completed the scheme of dark rich tones of sepia,

Above: The *Normandie* dining room: designed to seat seven hundred people, this grandiose room incorporated spectacular glass pillar lights by René Lalique and a large-scale bronze figure, "La Paix", by Dejean.

Right: The main lounge on the *Normandie*, decorated with murals of etched and painted glass by Jean Dupas.

black and gold. Equally arresting were the walls of Algerian onyx with decorations of hammered glass and gilded metalwork by Raymond Subes in the main entrance hall, the silver leaf walls of the theatre, claimed to be as large and as well equipped as many theatres in London and Paris, the 75-foot (23-metre) long swimming pool, the corridors lacquered in old rose and silver and the winter garden arranged by Mme de Vilmorin and Emile-Jacques Ruhlmann. Numerous ornate suites, consisting of drawing room, bedroom and dining room, were designed by the leading decorators of Paris and like the smaller state rooms featured walls covered in leather, woven straw, panels of etched glass or engraved metal, suggesting "some rich jewel casket rather than a prosaic bed-room". Two state rooms with metal walls and metal furniture were from the designs of Ruhlmann and of Mme Klotz. The decorations of the second- and tourist-class sections, though less sumptuous, were conceived on an equally grand scale and it is remark-able that throughout the liner the schemes were in the contemporary manner—only two of the private suites were in the eighteenth-century style.

The liner was deprived by a piece of pettifogging bureaucracy of a scheme which would have added to the richness of its decorations. Raoul Dufy was invited to ornament the walls surrounding the swimming pool with painted panels on any subject he might choose. It is tempting to imagine that he might have used the yachting themes he explored so brilliantly in many paintings and drawings and particularly in the

backcloth for the ballet *Beach*, a charming light *diver-tissement* choreographed by Léonide Massine to music by Jean Françaix which was presented by the Ballets de Monte Carlo in 1933. However, the ruling was that although Dufy had been decided upon to receive the commission, there must, for reasons which have been forgotten, appear to be some sort of open competition, of which Dufy would be the ostensible prize winner. He refused to take part in this charade, and the swimming pool was decorated by another hand.

It should be said that Dufy's pleasure in depict-ing the freshness and gaiety of yachts, brilliant sun-shine and the deep blue of a Mediterranean sea was marred by a degree of misfortune where boats were concerned. The large panels commissioned by Paul Poiret to decorate the three barges *Amours*, *Délices* and *Orgues* which were a feature of the Paris 1925 Exhi-

bition were met with such critical indifference that it is not possible to determine with accuracy the exact number of paintings. Indirectly, one of these panels was to affect the lives of one man and countless women. This panel, depicting a map of Paris, was bought from Poiret by a young man dabbling in art dealing. In the early thirties, desperately hard up, he sold his Dufy painting and with the money was able to exist until the time his fashion designs earned him sufficient to live upon. That young man's name was Christian Dior.

There is a certain irony in the statement in the commemorative booklet issue to mark the launching of the *Normandie*: "The French line were determined that their splendid new liner the *Normandie* should approach as nearly as possible to a 100 per cent fire proof ship . . . the possibility of catastrophe by fire on board this vessel is a very remote possibility." The *Normandie* caught fire in New York harbour in 1942, sank during the salvage operations, was raised after the war with a view to reconditioning but was found to be too damaged and was scrapped. Thus the most luxurious liner of its day terminated its short life of seven years.

ENGLAND

The situation as regards the decorative arts was rather different in England. The luxury exports to the United States were on a far smaller scale—for while Americans appreciated the tradition associated with England it was in France that they found the chic and elegance for which they yearned and which they were unable to find at home. The longer-term effects of the Wall Street Crash were on a more mundane level which affected the decorative arts indirectly. The general disorganizing of world markets brought about serious unemployment, and in addition in late 1929 the Australian government suspended all immigration, blocking a traditional escape route for those who could not find work in England. The various remedies attempted by English governments during the early thirties were ineffectual in stopping the downward trend which had reached such proportions that no

government could do anything really constructive, and the only results were reductions in prices and incomes, a lowering of production and a consequent rise in unemployment—a conservative figure of three million out of work was given. For most people these factors led to a considerably lower standard of living.

To prevent the drain of money abroad, tariffs of 10 per cent upwards were imposed on all imports except meat and wheat, a campaign to "buy British" was launched and attempts were made to improve the almost non-existent export trade. John de la Valette opened his introductory chapter to *The Conquest of Ugliness* with the statement that "The Glory of God and the joy of men are the constant sources of beauty. To extol the one and give voice to the other are the aims to which art aspires," but a more practical view can be observed in the preface by the Prince of Wales: "a greater attention to the artistic side of industry is essential if our manufacturers are to develop their domestic and overseas markets. Proof is not lacking that tariffs, however high, fail to keep foreign goods out of a country if they possess qualities which the domestic article lacks." The slogan of fitness for purpose had a sharply practical reason. The conquest of ugliness, "the introduction of decency and beauty into the lives of the people, especially at the lower end of the social scale" were admirable desires and John de la Valette's sincerity in formulating them should not be questioned, but the fact remains that behind the idealism lay the urgent necessity to sell more goods at home and abroad.

The picture dealers, jewellers, antiquaries and those working in other branches of the luxury trades were, as we have seen, among the first to feel the effects of the Depression and in their case the impact was immediate. However, many of them either had sufficient financial backing to tide them over for quite a while or they had enough clients unaffected by the Depression to enable them to keep in business even if on a reduced scale.

Among the worst hit were the studio craftsmen and the artworkers. Large numbers of these had set up in business after the war, eking out a day-to-day existence on slender financial resources and even more slender talents. Many of these were women.

Some had lost husbands or fiancés and were hoping to augment pensions or small private incomes by making and selling handicrafts; others were reluctant to relinquish the newly found independence they had experienced by working in factories or in the services during the war and equally hoped to earn a living even if they had no particular skills which would enable them to find a regular job in an overcrowded labour market. When, in about 1930, as the side-effects of the Crash began to be felt, there was a general decrease in spending, these handicraft workers and the shops selling their products found that there were fewer and fewer people able to buy hand-thrown pottery, painted lampshades, leathercraft or craft jewelry. At the same time the fashionable bare rooms—and this at least was a fashion people could afford to follow —dictated that the flat surfaces, tops of bookcases, tables, sideboards and other pieces of furniture should be free and uncluttered by a host of knick-knacks. Thus the creators and purveyors of these harmless trifles were added to the growing numbers of unemployed. Only the best craftsmen were able to survive and even they, during the thirties, had a hard struggle to keep going. When it is possible to discover the original price of a piece of pottery thrown and fired by a master craftsman the profit margin seems to have been negligible.

It needed a sense of complete dedication or a private income to keep head above water in these circumstances. In consequence there was no influx of new blood into the crafts which had already been diluted by amateurism in the twenties and brought into a somewhat contemptuous disrepute which found expression in the dismissive term "arty crafty", with its implications of homespun tweeds and morris-dancing, the latter a particular target for satire in revues during the thirties.

The confusion of design in the late twenties and early thirties can perhaps best be illustrated by citing the state of affairs in an actual decorating firm during that period. Established in the early years of the century, this firm in London had, like so many others, specialized in period reproduction designs of furniture and interior decoration. Patronized by royalty, it had had an impressive list of clients and its work had

been represented at all the important international exhibitions. The standard of craftsmanship was impeccable, which meant that a considerable number of pieces of reproduction furniture made in its workshops have since become "genuine antiques", including a version of an eighteenth-century pine-panelled room which eventually found a resting place in a museum. The design policy of the firm was controlled by the head of the drawing office who held the equivalent of the rank of director of the business. He had gained this position by seniority rather than by talent and during the twenties his staff numbered a dozen or more. By 1930 and the beginning of the Depression this had dwindled to four. Helped by the standard reference books, these draughtsmen could design and do the full-size drawings for a piece of furniture from any period from Elizabethan to late Georgian. Competent draughtsmen and versed in period ornament as they were, they had no interest at all in any other branch of the arts and, even if their long working hours had permitted, felt no urge to visit exhibitions of painting, sculpture or even contemporary industrial art. In the prosperous days of the twenties, in the unlikely event of a client expressing a wish for a modern scheme the salesman would either have talked him out of it or, if unsuccessful, have sent him elsewhere.

In the early thirties the picture had changed. Clients were few and far between and the financial position of the firm—even its existence—was threatened, for not many people could afford elaborate period schemes any longer. Modernism with its inexpensive simplicity was finding admirers whether through choice or necessity. This situation placed the drawing office of this firm in a dilemma. With no sympathy or training for Modernism the designers had to copy examples from the few available volumes of contemporary decoration—mostly dating from the Paris 1925 Exhibition. The simple built-in furniture presented few problems but if a panel of ornament was needed they had no precedent. Consequently motifs, Art Deco or geometrical, were borrowed from other sources and combined into a composition which was modern in that it had no references to the periods with which the draughtsmen were familiar. This case

The first-class lounge on the ss *Orion* (*above*), designed by Brian O'Rorke in 1934–35. Like the *Queen Mary* and the *Queen Elizabeth*, the liner was decorated in a subdued Modernist manner that never achieved the style or splendour of the contemporary French liners or even the Dutch *Nieuwe Amsterdam*. However, it did mark the mid-thirties break with the traditional "period" treatment, of which the smoking room of the *Viceroy of India* of 1929 (*right*) was a typical example, with its mock-Tudor panelling, plaster ceilings and false fireplaces.

of a real firm (with which the author had personal experience) was repeated many times elsewhere and the same circumstances applied to the firms of metalworkers, plasterers, woodworkers and decorative sculptors sub-contracted by architects, particularly on public buildings.

In firms such as these the design aspects of the work produced was firmly controlled by an older generation of draughtsmen and craftsmen who had entered the business before the First World War—even before 1900. Since then they had been turning out continually the same designs year after year, uninfluenced by fashion and completely unaware of developments on the Continent. With the coming of the Depression they retained their positions by virtue of long service, while junior members of the staff were dismissed or left of their own accord to branch out in other directions. Left with a staff unable to keep up with changing tasks, many of these firms foundered or were amalgamated with other concerns.

3
DECORATIVE STYLE FOR INTERIORS

MODERNISM ASSIMILATED

T he historicism which pervaded design in England during the twenties showed signs of giving way in about 1929 to influences from the Continent and in particular from France. The few exhibitions of French or French-inspired furniture at Shoolbred's and Waring and Gillow's had introduced English designers and public alike to a version of Art Deco diluted with the Modernism which was already superseding it on the Continent; and for a brief period there were indications of the beginnings of a distinctive English style in which the period references so dear to English taste were minimal though not entirely absent—a style which tended to dissipate as the effects of the Depression made themselves felt, though some designers, like Oliver Hill, were continuing to produce examples in this style even at the

end of the decade. The use of gold and silver leaf applied to walls and ceilings had been seen in the twenties; a range of certain colours in decoration, black, jade green, coral and lemon yellow, dated from the immediate post-war years, but these elements had hitherto been used in conjunction with period or reproduction furniture to create an effect which, charming in its own way, was still rooted in the past. The new feeling in the work of, for instance, Basil Ionides and Oliver Hill came from brilliant colour and specially designed furniture—even in some cases steel furniture—and a lavish use of mirrors, plain and coloured, and of metal foil. Period mouldings, cornices, dado rails or skirtings, hitherto regarded as necessary adjuncts, were either dispensed with completely or replaced with stepped mouldings or bands of fluting—a motif which in later and more austere designs became the sole relief from plain surfaces. There is, however, one motif which appears with variations in the work of a number of designers and in fact persists to the end of the thirties, particularly in association with mirrors. The contrasting curves found in the walnut frames of early eighteenth-century English mirrors and occasionally in the panelled doors of bureau-bookcases were imitated in the coloured mirror surrounds to decorative looking-glasses, and in some cases the tops of alcoves.

Left: The lounge at Claridge's hotel, London, decorated by Oswald P. Milne in 1930. The geometrically patterned black and cream carpet, specially commissioned from Marion Dorn, was the main element in a style of restrained Modernism—a compromise between Modernism and Art Deco, which was typical of a number of interiors created about 1930.

The renovation of "a gloomy Early Victorian building" at Cambridge by the Australian architect Raymond McGrath was a typical example of this style and received much critical acclaim in decorating magazines. Both the exterior and the interior of the house were transformed—with the exception of one or two of the original mantelpieces—into a tribute to a legendary Scottish queen, "Finella", "credited by tradition with having contrived a palace all of glass and having leaped to her death in a fathomless water-

fall". Beyond renaming the house "Finella" and incorporating a pool with a totem pole of concrete covered with Pictavian designs and carved with a double head of the queen from whose mouths jets of water sprang, the tribute was inconspicuous. A contemporary description of the entrance hall indicates the use of coloured glass and metal—"the mansard ceiling is of silvered ribbed cast glass of a jade green colour. The pointed arch which divides the silver-leafed vault from the hall proper springs from pilasters of cast glass lit from within, the axial door has a surround of gold mirror, the walls are silver leaf lacquered green, the floor is of black induroleum composition with a border of blue and a line of gold mosaic."

The two pink-walled living rooms were divided by folding doors faced with copper Plymax with large handles of black nickel, set in burnished silver-leafed architraves, while the architrave of another door was replaced by a surround of black glass. The staircase featured a contrast between lemon-yellow mirror and lavender doors.

The impersonality of the larger public rooms in hotels, which can so easily become portentous, was lightened by decorators working in this style by a lavish use of shaped and engraved mirrors whose glittering faceted reflections gave an impression of animation no matter how few people were in the rooms. Oswald Milne's schemes for Claridge's Hotel have become inevitably altered with the passage of time but enough remains to indicate the luxurious elegance which characterized them when they were new in the early thirties. The primrose walls, silver-grey cornices, ebonized woodwork, floors of Roman stone and black marble, the wrought-iron doors by Byron Inison incorporating glass panels by Lalique, and the boldly designed carpets contributed to a general effect eminently suitable for a luxury hotel. The compromise between Art Deco (elaborate mirror

Left: The entrance hall to Mansfield Forbes's house, Finella, in Cambridge, decorated by Raymond McGrath in 1929–30.

Right: A corner of the lounge at Claridge's by Oswald P. Milne, showing the combination of Modernist and Art Deco styles.

"drapery" and decorative lighting ornaments in wrought iron) and Modernism (a black-and-cream carpet by Marion Dorn with a geometrical design, angular treatment of two smaller mirror panels and a Cubist design of the furnishing fabrics) was typical of a number of interiors created about 1930 and can be compared with Oliver Hill's scheme for Gayfere House and Raymond McGrath's redecoration of Finella. The specially designed carpets and the lavish use of expensive materials and accessories were con-

ceived at a time before the effects of the Depression were being felt.

A bedroom designed by Elwes Ltd and illustrated in the *Studio Year Book of Decorative Art* for 1931 further demonstrates the use of metal foil and intense colour. The caption describes "walls hung with specially made paper in rich blue-green, mottled to represent Persian pottery: ceiling silver: floor black inlaid with silver: doors, mantelpiece and furniture of mirror. The bed is gold, hangings in blue-green shot

silk lined with cerise satin." Even this caption gives no idea of the elaboration of the four-poster bed which extended in height from a dais to the ceiling and had an intricately carved headboard, while the doors were ornamented with outlined vases with a scrolled ornament reminiscent of a Lalique scent bottle.

In another scheme of decoration for a house in London, Elwes Ltd combined the honey-brown walls of the dining room with "Italo-Spanish" furniture, stripped and waxed, brown carpet and curtains and table top, columns with urns for indirect lighting and a mantelpiece of imitation malachite. The walls of the drawing room were shaded from deep jade green at the skirting to pale green at the cornice and the furniture covered in gold fabric, while the bedroom had gold walls, gold, silver and brown fabrics, black mirrors, a cherry carpet and a ceiling painted to represent the midnight sky.

Darcy Bradell and Humphrey Deane, the architects of the Hon. Henry Mond's house, provided a variation on the style in the treatment of the dining room. *The Architectural Review* commented that "although the architectural ornament is of an academic pattern, the grouping and masses are not, so that the room as a whole cannot be described as a 'period' one. It has been built in direct contradiction to that school of modern decoration which owes its birth to the influence of the 'Ballet Russe'." The walls were sheathed in dull polished travertine marble carved with classic Greek ornament, the doors covered with sheet pewter studded with gilt *paterae* harmonizing with the massive nickel dining table by DIM placed on a cream rug with dark brown borders, the only ornaments being antique Greek sculpture and pottery, the only notes of colour the green horsehair coverings to the sycamore chairs. Concealed illumination in the cornice gave a range of lighting effects including that of moonlight.

OLIVER HILL

Of all the architect-designers working in this particular manner, and they included Guy Elwes, Basil Ionides, Edward Maufe, Symonds Lutyens and Lord Gerald Wellesley, the name of Oliver Hill occurs most frequently in the contemporary press. All the exhibitions

Left: The entrance hall to Gayfere House, London, designed by Oliver Hill for Lady Mount Temple in 1932. The sleek, contemporary, porcelain cats contrast with the T'ang dynasty guardian figures of demons placed on the radiator cases.

Below: The dining room at Mulberry House, London, designed by Darcy Braddell and Humphrey Deane for the Hon. Henry Mond in 1930.

Oliver Hill's own sitting room, decorated in about 1938, a rather late manifestation of the Modernist style. It is at its least austere, combining bookbindings and Chinese porcelain (on shelves set into the fireplace wall), a Chinese rug, fire-dogs of seventeenth-century design and exotic wood veneers. The white line drawings under plate glass on the chimney breast were by Eric Gill, and their near-eroticism recalls an incident over his sculpture of the naked figure of Ariel (modelled by the talented young actor Leslie French who had had a great success in the role): it had to be modified before it was unveiled as part of the decorations at the new Broadcasting House, London.

of the thirties devoted to design incorporated a major scheme by Oliver Hill—he designed the British Pavilion at the Paris 1937 Exhibition—and in addition he created for private clients numerous schemes varying in style from the luxurious to the expensively austere. His decorations in conjunction with Lady Mount Temple for Gayfere House were widely publicized throughout the thirties and here again an extensive use was made of mirrors. The bathroom in particular was the inspiration for many others on a less extravagant scale, and colour photographs appeared in a number of books on interior decoration. Its walls completely covered in grey mirror reflected a carefully placed collection of pale blue opaline glass, the floor was of black marble, the bath and wash basin of gold mirror with taps made of Lalique motor car mascots. It must have had considerable impact, especially when it was further decorated by vases of white madonna lilies.

Oliver Hill designed another bathroom at North House, Westminster, in a somewhat similar manner, with a marble bath, boldly fluted on the outside and lined with gold mosaic, set in an alcove defined with vertical strips of mirror. Grey mirror appears again in the dining room, used as architraves and other architectural features and accentuating the walls and the ivory-lacquered furniture. The walls were covered in white canvas, which was stencilled with green floral designs.

In a music room for Sir Albert Levy, Hill collaborated with the painter George Sheringham in a scheme which illustrated Hill's penchant for experimenting in new materials. Laminated wood was still regarded as a novelty and had hitherto been mainly used constructionally and painted or stained. In this case Hill used sheets of laminated wood, veneered with walnut, which extended from floor to ceiling with no pretence of their being "period" panelling but rather resembling large leaves of screens, an effect heightened by Sheringham's decorative paintings of Chinese scenes. Niches contained a collection of carved Chinese jades.

The more erotic aspects of the work of Eric Gill were given ample scope in Oliver Hill's own house. The Portland stone slabs incised with nudes by Gill, which decorated the dining room, had been adversely

The bathroom of North House, Westminster, London, designed by Oliver Hill in about 1931.

criticized when they were part of the Design in Industry Exhibition in 1935. The sitting room featured more of Gill's nudes; in this case they were drawn in white outline on the charcoal grey paper which covered the chimney breast and were protected by sheets of plate glass. A noticable feature of this room was the panelling of cedar wood with strongly marked grain in ivory colours. A built-in fitment enclosing a chaise-longue covered in bottle green velvet was veneered with macassar ebony and contained a radiogram. The ceiling was pale yellow, the curtains of grey-blue shot taffeta, and the room contained an antique Chinese rug with a yellow ground and a charcoal-coloured alcove displaying Chinese porcelain.

BASIL IONIDES

Basil Ionides, perhaps the most original of the designers working in this style, was given full scope for his fertile imagination in the decorations for the Savoy Theatre rebuilt on the site of a former theatre, uncomfortable and dilapidated, which had in its heyday been the home of the Gilbert and Sullivan operas. Raymond McGrath was full of praise for the completed theatre, writing to *The Architectural Review* that there were "two kinds of architecture—architecture which is lasting, simple and monumental in form and permanent in material, and architecture which is of the moment, accurate, impermanent. It is stupid to build decorated architecture to last and it is stupid to think that decorative art is not as important as that which is more monumental. Without fresh, vital, contemporary decoration everywhere, the public becomes artistically anaemic and unintelligent. . . . What we have got is our Savoy and its influence will be immeasurable without a doubt. A great many people will wake up in the morning and begin to rhapsodize about stainless steel or neon light and thus overnight are victories won."

If the opening of the theatre had not coincided approximately with the beginnings of the Depression, McGrath's prophecy as to the immeasurable influence of the Savoy decorations might have come true. But in the years to come there were few in a position to emulate the extravagance of the scheme. The auditorium was entirely covered in silver leaf lacquered in different shades of gold, the metallic sheen emphasizing the detail of the deep proscenium arch which projected and embraced the auditorium in a series of recessed panels enclosing modelled designs symbolic of the historic associations of the site. The seats and the curtain were in shades of red-brown, beige and coral, a gesture toward the traditional theatre colouring of red and gold. But before reaching this splendour the audience passed through the entrance doors, with bronze handles modelled by Gilbert Seale, into the foyer with its decorative light fittings (also by Gilbert Seale), its gold and silver carving and its decor of black marble and mirrors.

THE WHITEHALL AND CAMBRIDGE THEATRES

The Whitehall Theatre, built at the same time for the comedienne Marion Lorne by her husband Walker Hackett, occupied a much smaller site—the stage was one of the smallest and most awkward in London—but its decorations of silver leaf contrasted with black, red and green were no less elaborate than those of the Savoy. The architects, E. Stone and Partners, seem to have been inspired in the details by Swedish examples.

The new Cambridge Theatre, built by Wimperis,

Left: The façade of the Savoy Theatre, rebuilt in 1928–30 by the architects Easton and Robertson who collaborated with several designers.

The washroom (*above*) and the foyer (*above right*) of the Savoy Theatre. The main interior areas were designed by Basil Ionides; the decorative light fittings in the foyer were by Gilbert Seale.

Simpson and Guthrie and decorated by Serge Chermayeff, was equally lavish in its use of gold leaf, the curved interior of the auditorium being treated with gold of different shades, darkening in tone on the planes furthest from the proscenium. Compared with contemporary theatres the Cambridge was austere in its absence of decorative motifs in the auditorium but the clean lines and rich surface treatment—now unfortunately repainted—had a striking effect which did not, however, prevent criticism as to the lack of ornament.

These two theatres and the Savoy were examples of a type of contemporary decoration which had little or no reference to historic styles, but historicism triumphed in the Phoenix Theatre, built by Gilbert Scott, Crewe and Masey and decorated by Komisarjevsky. Here the decoration was relentlessly Italian Renaissance, incorporating facsimiles painted by Polunin of frescoes of the period.

The interior of the Gaumont Palace cinema, Cheltenham, in 1933.

Had the theatre managers had any idea of the grim times ahead of them it is doubtful whether these theatres would have been built or, if they had, whether the decorations would not have been on a more economic scale. Theatre had suffered from the advent of the silent film but over the years the situation had adjusted itself. Believing that nothing could replace the live theatre, theatre managers maintained the view that the talkies were a passing phase, a novelty of which the public would soon tire; and, considering the indifferent direction, acting and sound reproduction of the majority of the early talkies, there was some justification for this opinion. The new theatres, designed to attract the public away from the cinemas and to equal in magnificence the often over-blown decors of the big cinemas, were capable of being adapted into cinemas themselves in the worst eventuality—it so happened that those described remained as legitimate theatres. The Depression, however, began to make itself felt about the time these theatres opened and 1930 heralded a decade of economic stress for their owners.

OLIVER BERNARD

The late sixties dismantling of the entrance to the Strand Palace Hotel, a fantasy of decorative Modernism in marble, chromium and plate glass, drew attention to its designer, Oliver P. Bernard. His autobiography, *Cock Sparrow*, published in 1933 and written in the third person, ends at the close of the Great War but contains information about his early working years. Like Frank Brangwyn, Bernard spent a number of years as a sailor but his artistic training was gained as a theatrical scene painter and later as a designer for opera. Bernard was commissioned by Covent Garden and the Boston Opera House—it was on a trip to Boston that he survived the sinking of the *Lusitania* —mainly to design for productions of Wagner; a reproduction of a setting for Wagner's *Ring of the Nibelungs* was illustrated in *The Studio* for 1926. The accompanying caption records that Captain Oliver P. Bernard was "the decorator responsible for the most outstanding mural decorations (outdoor and indoor) at Wembley [the British Empire Exhibition of 1924] wherein he showed very great accomplishment as a colourist and evinced a happy fertility in humorous invention."

Bernard's training and experience of the theatre necessarily coloured his outlook when he came to the task of designing interiors for hotels and restaurants during the early thirties. Accustomed to creating a striking visual effect and then working out a method of translating this effect in terms of paint and canvas, he was less fettered by practical considerations than, for instance, an architect whose training, particularly in the period under discussion, generally tended to stifle any imaginative flights of fancy. Only a designer working in a theatrical tradition could have conceived the decoration of a restaurant (the Corner House, Tottenham Court Road, now demolished) in terms of walls covered with tapestry-like views of mountain scenery with pine forests and waterfalls carved out in differently coloured marbles. It was perhaps this theatrical element which made his work popular with the proprietors of the popular hotels and restaurants he designed—a larger-than-life bravura quality which turned anything from a cocktail to a banquet into a festive occasion in glamorous surroundings.

The entrance staircase from the street to the foyer of the Strand Palace Hotel with its illuminated glass balustrades was a smaller but more solid version of the staircase found in the final scenes of a revue at the Folies Bergère or the Casino de Paris, glittering settings for the descent of the star in sequins and ostrich plumes. His design for the Empire Room at the Trocadero Restaurant—also demolished—was rather more restrained, although his use of repeated arched openings, filled with peach-tinted glass and gilded bronze traceries, of walls faced with blond wood panelling and a dividing wall similarly decorated, which rose from the floor to partition the huge banqueting hall into two smaller but still spacious rooms, had a decorative exuberance rarely found among his more sober contemporaries.

DECORATORS AND ENSEMBLIERS

Raymond Cogniat, in an article on the decorative arts written in 1932 for the magazine *L'Amour de l'Art*, put forward the theory that during the nineteenth century the decoration of interiors was dominated by cabinet-makers and upholsterers, in 1920 by dressmakers and in 1930 by architects. This was certainly true at the time Cogniat wrote his article, though architects were to be ousted from their leading positions in a very few years' time, to be replaced by designers for the theatre, dressmakers and the new generation of interior decorators.

During the thirties the rapidly changing social conditions brought about the end of the monopoly of the decorating profession by the big firms of furnishers and decorators and the triumphant rise of a new profession—that of interior decorator. In the previous decade voices had been raised, notably those of contributors to *The Studio*, deploring the influence over their clients of the salesmen in the big firms, salesmen dependent upon augmenting a minimal wage by commission on sales. With a vested interest in selling antique furniture, whether genuine or reproduction, and in persuading their clients to order ex-

pensive panelling and elaborate plasterwork as a setting for their furniture, they were naturally the enemies of any innovations in style. In the hard times of the thirties, these big establishments found it increasingly difficult to maintain their overheads, with the consequence that the staffs in the drawing offices, as well as the less persuasive salesmen, found themselves redundant. Many of these drifted into other forms of employment or to a life on the dole, but the younger and more adventurous ones with small capital set up as freelance decorators. Added to these were young people with artistic leanings who ordinarily might have become painters or sculptors but with hardly anyone buying pictures or sculptures by established names, let alone by unknown beginners, interior decoration offered an attractive alternative. Rents were low and premises with good addresses readily available. The requirements were few: a good appearance—ugly interior decorators had to rely upon talent—a fund of small talk, the ability to last out at interminable cocktail parties and a reputation for that mythical quality "natural good taste", which was regarded as a substitute for ability. The rewards could be an active social life, a circle of wealthy clients and even a rich wife or husband. These decorators were described in 1932 by Paul Nash as "charming young men and formidable ladies . . . hopping backwards and forwards between England and the Continent on the benefit of the Exchange. In their homeward flight they seldom failed to carry back something for the nest, a piece of stuff from Paris, a German lamp, a steel chair or just a headful of other people's ideas."

If these charming young men and formidable ladies had some ability for drawing and painting they could alternatively earn a meagre living as decorative artists under the patronage of interior decorators, or dealing directly with their clients. As few interior decorators could draw, let alone design, there was always a need for renderings in watercolour of pro-

posed schemes of decoration or of single pieces of furniture to give the client an approximate idea of the finished result. Others existed by painting furniture with decorative floral arrangements or with landscapes, especially in the later thirties when honest pieces of Victorian furniture were painted in the fashionable pastel shades, decorated with baroque motifs and treated to give a *craquelure* or crazing to the paint. There was also the occasional commission to paint a four-fold screen with a design in the manner of Rex Whistler, but the fashion for silk lampshades painted with a reproduction of the design on the *famille rose* or Meissen vase converted into a lampstand had, in the main, died with the twenties.

If anything Paul Nash made an understatement in using the word "formidable" to describe the women interior decorators. The generation of women who in the post-war years had been desperately and hopefully trying to earn a living from the decorative arts were mostly inexperienced in business and totally unprofessional, gentlewomen to the last with their sad leather bookmarks, pixie ornaments made out of pine cones, powder bowls decked with barbola flowers, rolled-paper bead necklaces and photograph frames decorated with swirls of sealing wax. There were a few skilled craftswomen whose talents were considerable enough to enable them to survive into the thirties: Stella Crofts, who modelled vigorous and unsentimental animals in pottery; the textile printers Dorothy Larcher, Enid Marx and Phyllis Barron; Sybil Dunlop, whose silver jewelry set with multi-coloured semi-precious stones had echoes of the Italian Renaissance and Ashbee's Guild of Handicraft, and Dorrie Nossiter whose jewels were described as "poetry made precious". But these were exceptional and the majority of the pathetic, courageous figures had faded with the twenties. In their place appeared a new generation of lady decorators who, from necessity as much as inclination, developed qualities of toughness that would have embarrassed Attila. Some had social connections through birth or marriage, some, even more advantageously, had titles, but all had an unshakable belief in their own taste and talent. Ruthless with their clients, they were often completely unscrupulous in their dealings with the cabinet-

Left: The interior of 35 Cliveden Place in 1938, designed by Oliver Hill in a luxurious version of the Modernist style. The austerity of the polished stone walls is relieved by incised decoration of stylized naked figures.

makers, upholsterers, painters and other technicians they employed—craftsmen who in the hard days of the thirties could not afford to offend, no matter how often requests for settlement of long-outstanding bills were loftily ignored. Woe betide a client who bought anything from a rival decorator—by the lift of an eyebrow they could insinuate that the object was a shoddy fake, an error of taste, absurdly expensive and that the morals of the rival decorator were highly suspect.

The rivalry and mutual distrust between decorators at this period can be summed up in a true story in which the protagonists must, of necessity, remain anonymous. A celebrated woman decorator, whom we will call X, had her premises immediately opposite those of another decorator, Y. Finding her stock of choice pieces of decorative furniture running low, X would on occasion cross the road and in Y's absence choose some of his best pieces to the tune of, say, £1000 and they would immediately be transferred to her own showroom. Knowing perfectly well from past experience that X had little or no intention of paying without actually being sued, Y would, in his turn, wait until X had gone to lunch and then select from her stock items to the value of £1100, leaving a cheque for the difference.

Paul Nash's comment about "a headful of other people's ideas" pinpoints a problem which became increasingly pressing after 1932. For professional reasons a decorator was anxious to have a recently completed scheme, whether for one room or a whole house, featured at some length in one or more of the prestige magazines. The editors of these journals were only too glad to collaborate if the work had been done for a celebrity, as they found that their readers gained a vicarious pleasure from a peep into the homes of the famous—it was during the late twenties and thirties that it became socially acceptable for titled women to endorse beauty products in fashion magazines, for a fee. But at the same time readers took these pictures to their decorators with the request that a piece of furniture, a fabric or decorative effect should be copied and, as a result, the first decorator and his client found to their dismay that original creations were being widely and often badly plagiarized.

THE ARCHITECTURAL REVIEW COMPETITION OF 1930

During the twenties the profession of interior decorator in the sense of one who specializes in designing or choosing the decorations, furnishings and lighting in agreement with the client, whether for a new building or for an old one, was too new a concept for most architects to accept with any seriousness. Many architects of an older generation specializing in domestic design were also given the responsibility for the design of the interiors by their clients. Alternatively, it was entrusted to designers attached to the big decorating firms—this was especially the case where the fashionable reproduction period panelling was concerned. As for furniture, the clients would either possess all that was necessary, whether genuinely antique or, as was more likely, reproduction, or they could order it from one of the big firms. The post-war boom in low-priced building brought a new generation of architects whose main interest was confined to the external appearance of the house and, in making a pleasing arrangement of windows or other architectural features on the outside, they often paid little attention to the effects such a treatment might have on the inside. In a neo-Georgian house, for example, a formal drawing room could have the windows or doors asymmetrically and awkwardly arranged, the chimney breast could be out of centre or—a very common occurrence—the windows placed right in the corner of the room with no room left for curtains. Rarely if ever was there any consultation between the architect and the interior designer before the plans were finalized.

The purpose underlying the competition announced in *The Architectural Review* in May 1930 was to interest architects in the practical aspects of interior decorating and also in the possibilities of using the work of contemporary designer-craftsmen, some of whom had had a struggle to survive during the twenties and whose working existence was threatened by the Depression.

Rarely has a competition stipulated so many conditions for the entrants to contend with, though, as will be seen, the rules were not too strictly observed.

However, the prizes of £100, £50 and £25 were considerable inducements in 1930 and in addition the prizewinners were promised the prestige and publicity of having their designs built and exhibited in Waring and Gillow's showrooms. The competitors were required to design the decorations and furnishings for a drawing room and adjoining dining room (which could be either separate or combined in one large room) for an imaginary client, Lord Benbow, a Clydeside shipbuilder ennobled for his public services to the City of Glasgow. The rooms were to be part of his London home in bachelor apartments near Curzon Street where on occasions his sister acted as hostess, his lordship being a widower.

Born in a London suburb some sixty years before, Lord Benbow had spent many years in Glasgow and was thus acquainted with the work of Charles Rennie Mackintosh, though this enthusiasm for the work of the Glasgow school had changed into a devotion for the later developments of the Modern Movement. Here it must be pointed out that it was unusual to consider in 1930 that the work of Charles Rennie Mackintosh was something to be admired. In order to spread his patronage as widely as possible Lord Benbow wished to commission several artists to collaborate. Some furniture by Thomas Hope might be incorporated; and, as Lord Benbow was the owner of a stud farm and a racing stable, the portrait of a Derby winner could be included as well. It was hoped that

Paul Nash's design for the "Lord Benbow" competition, which won the second prize.

the effect achieved would be "gracefully sporting".

The conditions of the competition have been quoted at length since they reflect the common tendency of the time to accuse interior decorators of designing schemes lacking in personality or which were in accordance with the decorator's taste rather than that of the client. This was undoubtedly true of some of the Modernistic interiors of the early thirties, but with the imaginary Lord Benbow the organizers of the competition posed problems that would have taxed the ingenuity of the most experienced professional designer.

Any hopes that new talents would be discovered were dashed when the announcement was finally made, for the first, second and third prizewinners were all designers whose names and work were very familiar to regular readers of the journal, though only the first had had any architectural training, the others being painters and textile designers.

The first prize was awarded to Raymond McGrath, whose scheme included rugs by McKnight Kauffer, fabrics by Paul Nash, paintings and wallpapers by Edward Bawden and sculpture by Maurice Lambert. The jury made little comment on what was a pleasant but not outstanding conception which, like the designs of the other prizewinners, made only the slightest acknowledgment to the tastes of Lord Benbow.

Paul Nash's second-prizewinning design with furniture and fittings by Denham Maclaren, paintings by Edward Wadsworth and textiles by Paul Nash, received the comment that it was a "design made faintly ridiculous by the fact that the artist either misunderstood the purpose of the remarks regarding Lord Benbow's sporting tastes or surrendered to his sense of humour". Certainly the treatment of the doors, the wall brackets in the shape of cricket stumps made from tubular lights, the electric radiator disguised as a football, the armchairs designed as cricket pads and the folding screens of tennis netting suggest Nash had his tongue in his cheek. Here again there is no sign of the Derby winner, the Thomas Hope furniture, or Charles Rennie Mackintosh.

The choice of the scheme submitted by Vanessa Bell in collaboration with Duncan Grant for the third

prize is surprising in view of the editorial comment that "the competitor has shown a still greater contempt for the plan produced by Lord Benbow and one feels that with very little alteration the same scheme could be carried out in almost any kind of room." Mrs Bell's decor, with carpets and curtains by Humphrey Slater, sculpture by John Skeaping and furniture and light fittings by Robert Medley, was more reminiscent of Bloomsbury than Mayfair, of the Omega Workshops than the racing stable, and it goes without saying that in this scheme also there was no provision made for the portrait of the Derby winner. After the bare announcement of the winners' names and the comments of the judges, *The Architectural Review* seems to have considered the matter closed and there is no record of the winning designs ever having been built or exhibited.

"THE 1930 LOOK IN BRITISH DECORATION"

Also in 1930, *The Studio* took a more practical step by giving its readers a summary of "The 1930 Look in British Decoration", featuring the work of three decorators, each working in a completely different manner from the others and each with an individual approach to the subject.

The designs of Francis Bacon, described as "a young English decorator who has worked in Paris and in Germany for some years and is now established in England", were demonstrated by photographs of his studio, "formerly an uninteresting garage", and now completely transformed with its windows curtained in white rubber sheeting. The furniture, its horizontal accents marked by long tubular steel handles somewhat reminiscent of towel rails, was painted in shades of grey with tops of black and white glass and shows the influence of De Stijl. The two large unframed circular mirrors lit by tubular glass bulbs were probably the forerunners of the many circular mirrors incorporated in Modernistic dressing tables during the thirties. The tubular steel stools and tables with circu-

Right: The design by Raymond McGrath that won first prize in *The Architectural Review* "Lord Benbow" competition of 1930.

lar tops of half-clear, half-mirror glass had a chill chic and brought to mind the caption under a photograph of steel furniture in an advertisement published by Heals in 1930: "Suggested ideas for the Highbrow". Displayed on the walls were rugs designed by Bacon in tones of grey, beige, brown and black—handsome rugs described as owing nothing to traditional or oriental styles, "they are purely thought forms".

In contrast to this was "a room of outstanding beauty, rich in colour, harmonious in design", the dining room decorated by Duncan Grant and Vanessa Bell for Lady Gerald Wellesley. Mainly grey in colouring, the room had six large panels with two smaller panels flanking the fireplace, freely painted with alcoves in which nude adults and children were grouped. The octagonal table, the chairs and the mantelpiece were decorated in characteristic designs and borders of coloured spots and circles. It cannot be said that these paintings were Duncan Grant's most successful works: the painted alcoves are too low for their width, with the consequence that the figures fit uncomfortably into them.

Above left: Francis Bacon's scheme, featured in "The 1930 Look in British Decoration" in *The Studio* of that year. The seat of the metal-framed stool is of black and white calfskin.

Left: The dining room created by Duncan Grant and Vanessa Bell, shown in *The Studio* of 1930. The central wall painting conceals a serving hatch.

Right: Modernist interior by David Pleydell-Bouverie, 1930.

Serge Chermayeff's sitting room and dining room, shown in *The Studio* of 1930.

ended cocktail cabinet. A mural by Alexander Bayes on a theme popular in the early thirties as an appropriate one for Modernist interiors—that of the skyscraper of a city of the future—filled the wall over the flush electric fire. An interesting contrast was provided by the dominant horizontal of the figured wood and the circular motifs of the rugs, the lampshades and the small table. The dining room, which could become a part of the other room when the large sliding doors were open, had plain walls and tubular steel chairs.

This contrast between rectangular shapes and circles was seen again in a room designed by David Pleydell-Bouverie dating from 1930, a room which, like so many of the period, gave the impression that its purpose was to be perpetually filled with people drinking cocktails, the women in sleek bias-cut dresses outlining the figure and ornamented solely by a pair of geometrical diamond clips, the men in dinner jackets with smooth brilliantined hair and a Bulldog Drummond air of weariness from a long day playing polo. Everything was reduced to a basic simplicity, the design of the walnut furniture pared down to essentials with even the grain of the veneers selected for its lack of exoticism; plain tweed upholstery repeated the deep amber of the walls but in a slightly darker tone. What might have resembled the impersonality of a superior dentist's waiting room was, however, brought to life by the bold design of McKnight Kauffer's carpets which brought together the rectangular and circular shapes of the tables and chairs in a geometrical composition carried out in dark brown, beige and sand.

ARUNDELL CLARKE

It would have been difficult for the plagiarist to find much to copy in the few photographs which appeared in periodicals advertising the interiors designed by Arundell Clarke. It is recorded that he exhibited his designs at the Ideal Home Exhibition of 1930 under the name of "Charm", an inappropriate pseudonym which he soon abandoned. His original premises were situated at 71 Royal Hospital Road, Chelsea, but a growing clientele enabled him to make a move to a more modish address, 18 Bruton Street, Mayfair, where an all-white showroom displayed the widely

The third scheme, representing another aspect of British decoration, was the sitting room and dining room designed for his own home by Serge Chermayeff, the Director of the Modern Art Department at Waring and Gillow's. This was a conversion of what appears to be the ground floor of an early Victorian house, the two rooms separated by sliding doors veneered in walnut, with the grain horizontal as in the rest of the fitted cupboards and the ubiquitous round-

publicized "Arundell Clarke Easy Chair" capable, it was claimed, of accommodating five people at one time, two on each broad arm and one unfortunate person in the usual seat. This elephantine chair was sold in considerable numbers, covered in the currently fashionable "amusing" fabrics, off-white sailcloth or plain heavy cotton or woollen fabrics dyed dark brown, ice blue or navy blue, the last a colour much favoured by Arundell Clarke. Another speciality was a large square ashtray of cast glass.

The text of an Arundell Clarke advertisement widely published in 1933 is worth quoting as a reflection of the scarcity of money at the time: "There are people who think that because the modern style of furnishing is so beautiful it must therefore be expensive. Nothing could be further from the truth. Modern design gets its lovely effect from the use of space and light and an intense simplicity of form and textures. I could furnish an entire 'modern' room for what the Victorians would have spent on curtains and carpets alone! Write for my new catalogue or call. My shop is open until 7 o'clock." The accompanying photograph shows the corner of a white room (actually one of the showrooms) entirely devoid of any mouldings, a bare polished floor, the windows draped with rather skimpy unlined curtains, the only furniture being a settee and one of the famous armchairs covered in white material, and a small plain table supporting a baluster-shaped china vase adapted as a lamp with a plain metallic shade. The only break in this almost monastic severity is offered by an arrangement of white lilies. Such a scheme was obviously Arundell Clarke's personal concept of the perfect interior and one which he was able to persuade some of his clients to commission, but judging from other examples of his work he was obliged to conform to the more general demand for built-in furniture, simple in outline and veneered with the decoratively grained woods so much in use. This aspect of his work was featured on a number of occasions by the German magazine *Innen Dekoration* edited by Alexander Koch. He and Ian Henderson were the only two English decorators of note whose work was examined in this periodical during the thirties; the French decorator Jean Royère was also the subject of several articles.

CURTIS MOFFAT

In 1929 Curtis Moffat, an American photographer who had spent a considerable time in Paris, opened premises at 4 Fitzroy Square, London, a Georgian house which was modernized by the architect Frederick Etchells. The opening was marked by the issuing of an invitation card designed by McKnight Kauffer and the announcement that Curtis Moffat would henceforth be the London representative of DIM (Décoration Intérieure Moderne). Apart from a number of announcements in the press, no mention of DIM was made in subsequent publicity or in the numerous magazine articles which were written by Derek Patmore and others so it seems likely that hopes in this direction were disappointed.

Curtis Moffat's intention was to combine the most *avant-garde* decoration with Gothic and Renaissance furniture and objects and, perhaps most significantly, with African tribal sculpture, of which he was an enthusiastic and knowledgable collector. Other collectors of such art shared Curtis Moffat's opinion that its best setting was a contemporary one. The collector Ladislas Szecsi tried a number of styles from Louis XV to early Victorian as backgrounds for the collection of primitive masks he had amassed in Africa before coming to the conclusion that they "are only in keeping in a modern environment. The mask being primarily a functional object is in harmony with furniture which is also functional, unbiased by aesthetic theory and without useless ornament." In order to interest the widest public, the advertisements for the new gallery were carefully calculated to appeal to the readers of the various magazines—illustrations of a carved jade vase or an Italian shrine for the staider journals, and photographs of a gleaming glass abstraction for periodicals like *Vogue* and *The Architectural Review* which, in their own separate ways, were abreast of the fashions.

The opening was widely reported in the gossip columns and the adjectives "Modernistic", "Cubist" and "Futuristic" applied to the white rooms with doors faced in aluminium or copper, the curtains made of squares of chamois leather hanging from polished nickel rods, the profusion of modern

Left: Invitation card designed by E. McKnight Kauffer for the opening of the Curtis Moffat shop on 4 June 1929.

Right: Interior by John Duncan Miller, 1937; the hand-tufted rug is by Ashley Havinden, and the chair on the left by C. Kendrick.

Below right: Interior created by John Duncan Miller for the Dorland Hall Exhibition of 1933, in some ways a dress rehearsal for the larger exhibition at Burlington House two years later, in which the Design and Industries Association played a leading part. The exhibits were conceived in a striking manner to drive home to the public and manufacturers alike the message that better design must be applied to interior furnishings if Britain's exports were to improve.

cushions in geometric patterns of velvet or coloured leather, the steel furniture and the African masks or bronze heads from Benin. Anyone who found the juxtaposition of a flower piece by Marie Laurencin in a faceted mirror frame and a carved wood figure from the Solomon Islands disturbing was reassured by a room with lettuce-green walls where ship models, antique leather drinking vessels and terrestrial globes were displayed.

Fitzroy Square and the neighbouring streets had been "discovered" in the 1920s and a number of social celebrities lived nearby. Curtis Moffat and his first wife, Iris Tree, the daughter of Sir Herbert Tree, were enthusiastic party-givers—Lytton Strachey was severely frightened by a snake at one of their parties —and it was not long before a trip to the Curtis Moffat gallery became a necessity if a birthday or Christmas

present was needed. A wide choice could be found from rugs by McKnight Kauffer at 4 guineas each; platinum, white gold, lacquer and diamond jewelry by Raymond Templier; "amusing china animals by Robert Lallemand"; cigarette boxes covered in leopard skin; metal cocktail sets by Desny, or cupboards painted by Wyndham Lewis who may have been reminded of his comment on "the amateur tasteful-ness of the Fitzroy tinkerers", made in 1919 about the earlier venture in the same neighbourhood—the Omega Workshops.

Occasional exhibitions were held of carpets by Marion Dorn, rugs by Evelyn Wild, furniture by Eyre de Lanux and Raymond Templier jewelry. Commissions for interior decorations were solicited in an advertisement in *Harper's Bazaar* in October 1930 with the injunction to the reader to "Go into these rooms

Design for a dining room by Curtis Moffat with furniture in walnut and metal by John Duncan Miller.

. . . you can breathe there and walk about . . . no longer decoration sickly with charm from which the spirit turns . . . here there is nothing of deception . . . the lie is a true one . . . the machine works."

In 1930 Curtis Moffat designed the settings and supplied the furniture for two comedies, *Healthy Wealthy and Wise* starring an American actress, Mary Newcomb, and *It's a Boy* with Leslie Henson and Sydney Howard. The female impersonation scene by the two stars of the latter ensured a good run but Curtis Moffat was the only one to emerge with credit from *Healthy Wealthy and Wise*, an unamusing effort.

Curtis Moffat added a picture gallery to his decorating business—a venture commended as show-

ing, in a way that no other gallery did, the function of pictures as furniture. Among the artists represented at the opening in January 1931 were Augustus John and Eve Kirk, for whose first exhibition John had written a glowing foreword to the catalogue. Eve Kirk's special genre was depicting, in a restricted range of cerulean blue, ochre and indian red, scenes of the Thames docks and—inevitably—Venice, with the paint laid on in a thick impasto applied with a palette knife and drawn over with a brush handle. John's admiration for her work was shared by a number of critics and she was described in 1931 as gradually establishing a position as one of the most important women painters in England.

The name John Duncan Miller appears at an early date in association with Curtis Moffat. He draughted designs for decorative schemes, wrote articles for magazines on various aspects of decoration, and designed the Marquis de Casa Maury's apartment in a style of modified Modernism. The fireplace wall of the drawing room was covered in sheets of mirror, reflecting the sky blue walls and ceiling and upholstery in shades of aquamarine and sapphire blue. The dining room had white walls and ceiling and dining chairs of Queen Anne design covered in aquamarine blue, while the top of the dining table was of thick pavement glass with a greenish cast of colour, a kind of glass much used by Curtis Moffat and other designers in the early thirties for table tops. The main feature of the dining room—and one much commented upon in the press—was the treatment of the curtains which were entirely covered in bronze, gold and silver sequins. "Escape from convention is one of the main features of the furnishing fabrics of this second quarter of the twentieth century," wrote Olive Dent in the introduction to the catalogue of the 1930 Daily Mail Ideal Home Exhibition. "Glittering sequinned material in geometrical patterns and two shades of gold acts as window hangings in one Mayfair drawing room."

The Curtis Moffat venture lasted a bare three years but during that time its influence was considerable. Run on unorthodox and uncommercial lines —factors which caused its eventual demise—it brought to the notice of the public experimental work which would never have had a showing elsewhere. Its closure was brought about partly by the Depression and partly by Curtis Moffat's desire to devote his time completely to his first interest, photography.

SYRIE MAUGHAM

Syrie Maugham's name is invariably associated with all-white schemes and she is usually credited with inventing the idea of colourless rooms. Doubts and even forceful denials have since been expressed by contemporaries and certainly white rooms were being done by other decorators, including Arundell Clarke and Jean-Michel Frank, at the same time, though the difficulty, if not impossibility, of establishing the exact dates when comparable white schemes were completed leaves the question a matter of speculation. What can be established is that Basil Ionides in *Colour and Interior Decoration* in 1926 was giving advice about schemes which combined white or ivory walls, paintwork and ceilings with white or black floors, white curtains of satin, bolton sheeting or alpaca, white horsehair upholstery and ornaments and lamps of Leedsware, white Wedgwood, *blanc de Chine* and white opaque glass. Ionides, in the introduction to a chapter on white rooms, commented that with the improvement of modern paints, enamels and distempers, "the old saying that white decoration is the last resort of people with no taste can no longer be accepted as true". From the evidence of many with first-hand information the impression is gained that Mrs Maugham was more of an impresario than an originator, combining a flair for adaptation with an acute sense of publicity.

Harper's Bazaar devoted an article in October 1929 to her Chelsea house, and Pollard Crowther illustrated it with soft-focus photographs reminiscent of those of Baron de Meyer—also a contributor to this particular issue. Entitled "Mrs Somerset Maugham's White House", the article describes the music room as having white walls, white satin curtains, white satin slip covers to the furniture, white lilies, white velvet lampshades and a pair of white porcelain camellia trees about four feet (1.25 metres) high, "the joy of the owner's heart and the envy of her friends". A corridor was enlivened with sheets of antique mirror and green-and-white painted wall hangings—a scheme almost duplicating one by Oliver Hill at North House. The stripped and waxed pine panelling of the dining room with its rock crystal appliques was a setting for white-painted chairs, the dining table being covered to the floor with an ivory fillet lace tablecloth upon which were arranged white flowers and white porcelain —Mrs Maugham brought back into fashion knives and forks with white porcelain handles. The furniture shown in the illustrations to *Colour and Interior Decoration, Simple Schemes for Decoration* by John Gloag and

Entrance hall designed by Syrie Maugham in about 1939, in which she has deviated rather markedly from her declared principle of elimination. Every piece appears to have been ruthlessly repainted, and the dolphin console table has been provided with a faceted mirror top. The bold stripes of the moiré wallpaper and the profusion of furniture and ornaments indicate that Syrie Maugham had abandoned the simplicity of her all-white period.

various articles in women's magazines of the twenties is invariably either "brown" furniture—that is, of polished wood—or nondescript pieces of painted furniture of no particular character. Syrie Maugham conformed to this general pattern in the decors mentioned, except that some of the pieces were of Continental origin and the brown furniture, like the panelling, was stripped and waxed.

Mrs Maugham's all-white drawing room which received considerable publicity in 1933 had more of the modern atmosphere, with its long plain settees upholstered in beige satin, a modern rug with a raised pile in a key pattern woven in two tones of cream by Marion

Dorn and a striking tall screen made of very narrow panels of mirror set in chromium-plated frames. Three Louis XV chairs, painted and upholstered in off-white, formed a group round a backgammon table and the problems of dealing with the grand piano was partly solved by concealing it behind a low eight-fold screen lacquered white. "Such a scheme is practical and need not be expensive," wrote Derek Patmore in *Colour Schemes for the Modern Home*, although the practicability of such a white room in London could be doubted and the mirror screen which gave so much character to the room could not have been particularly inexpensive. According to one person who had acquaintance

with it, this screen was a hazardous piece of decoration as the composition holding the long thin strips of mirror in position tended to melt if the room became warm, and pieces of glass would fall off without any warning.

Although Mrs Maugham's interiors were often described as including dead white and cream, these two shades were, according to a former colleague, anathema to her and during the all-white phase (which, in fact, lasted only a comparatively short time) she used every variation of white—ivory, pearl, oyster, parchment etc.—except the hard and unflattering dead white, or cream with its associations of suburbia.

Oliver Messel's design for the bedroom scene in Charles Cochran's *Helen!*, 1932: executed entirely in white, as was most of the show, it caused a sensation by its originality and elegance. A new presentation of Offenbach's *La Belle Hélène*, with lyrics by A. P. Herbert, choreography by Léonide Massine and produced by Max Reinhardt, it was one of the most notable productions of the decade, giving Oliver Messel a full-scale opportunity to design in the baroque tradition of the Bibbiena family.

"Elimination is one of the secrets of successful decoration," Syrie Maugham is quoted as saying in an article in *The Studio* in 1933 but it was not a precept to which she adhered too strongly. With a staff and overheads, any interior decorator bent on eliminating everything unnecessary from a decorative scheme is headed for financial ruin—even Jean-Michel Frank's apparent simplicity masked a use of expensive materials. As the thirties advanced Mrs Maugham's interiors tended to become more and more filled with decorative furniture and ornaments which were charming and fantastic but were really superfluous, for instance the shell groups made by the Comtesse Hervé de la Morinière for which Syrie Maugham was the London agent in 1937. These were composed of several large polished seashells with clusters of smaller shells fixed into the group with green-tinted plaster and could be used as decorative centrepieces for dining tables, and for little else. They were however soon copied in quantity and enjoyed a considerable vogue.

In 1932 the white craze reached its height—a craze epitomized in the look of the film star Jean Harlow, who appeared to have been constructed of equal parts of snow, marble and marshmallow. White beach wear was *de rigueur* for holidays on the Riviera and white evening dresses formed the greater part of the Paris collections. Oliver Messel's white decors and especially the baroque bedroom scene were a sensation in *Helen!*, a memorable presentation by C. B. Cochran of Offenbach's *La Belle Hélène*.

By 1934 the all-white room had gone out of fashion, according to a writer in *The Architectural Review*. In that year Mrs Maugham sold her house at Le Touquet and concentrated on the interior decorating business which since about 1930 had been at 2 Wyndham Place, Davies Street, and finally moved in 1934 to Paradise Walk, Chelsea. For the next five years she was extremely active and extended her range to the creation of a number of pieces of furniture which became identified with her name. Painted in various colours, ivory with the mouldings picked out in pale pink, a deep green with white mouldings, indigo blue

Left: Syrie Maugham's drawing room in shades of white, Chelsea, London, 1933.

and a dark orange approximately the colour called tango in the twenties, they had an artificial *craquelure* finish.

The forms of these different pieces of furniture were inspired by those of the simpler pieces of eighteenth-century French furniture sometimes called "provincial", but usually of an extremely elegant outline, simply executed with little or no carved decoration and left in the natural fruitwood or painted—furniture similar to that made by Nicolas Petit or Criaerd in the mid eighteenth century. Side tables with shelves and a drawer, sometimes with two zinc containers sunk in the top to take flowering plants; a triangular version of the same intended to fill the corner between a settee and another chair; bedside tables with a space for a tray and a raised part upon which a lamp could be placed; commodes based on Régence models with two drawers or with the drawer space left open to take large books; a finely detailed stand for a telephone with two lower compartments for directories—these were some of the models which became known as a "Syrie Maugham" signature to a room.

No doubt these simple models were chosen in preference to the more ornate pieces veneered in marquetry designs and ornamented with bronzes because they were less expensive to make. Also, taste in the thirties tended to turn away from the elaborate Louis XV and Louis XVI furniture as being vulgar and showy—a criticism justified in the majority of cases. Such furniture was a drug on the market whether genuine or, as was more likely, reproduction of the kind almost mass-produced about 1900. Many decorators inspired by the example of what Lord Berners called "Syrie Maugham's white furniture traffic" stripped off the bronzes and painted the carcasses of these inexpensive pieces of furniture. One genuine Régence commode had its inlaid marquetry panels covered in thick white paint and its rouge marble top similarly treated—fortunately the bronzes, of a very high quality, were put back. Such an instance could be multiplied a hundred times at a period when antiques of certain periods were so plentiful and so cheap. An Aubusson carpet, at that time easily obtained and inexpensive although coming back into fashion, had

its white background dyed violet by one new owner who applied household paint with disastrous results.

Mrs Maugham could hardly be blamed for the indiscretions of her imitators, though the poorly conceived copies of her white rooms undoubtedly influenced her to adopt more colourful schemes as the decade advanced. In 1936 *Vogue* recorded that Christian Bérard decorated Mrs Maugham's apartment but, although it would have been interesting to see the results of a collaboration between two people so influential in dictating taste during the thirties, no details of these decorations appear to have survived.

In addition to the individual pieces of furniture which were immediately recognizable as being Syrie Maugham creations, she had several characteristic treatments which were repeated time and time again. One was the use of fringe—a fairly long eyeglass fringe—where a gimp or braid would normally be used, for instance outlining the curves of a pelmet or around the arms of a sofa. Another was the use of a

crackled finish on the paintwork of furniture. Mrs Maugham employed one craftsman in particular who specialized in producing this finish of crazing the surface of the paint, the minute cracks being filled in with black or a coloured pigment, an effect resembling the *craquelure* of some Chinese porcelains. The work was carried out in a cloak and dagger atmosphere of locked rooms and great secrecy, the craftsman not allowing even Mrs Maugham to discover the mysteries of his technique. He was not unique in producing this crackled effect but his particular secret was in knowing how to control the size of the crazing of the paint. When Mrs Maugham closed her establishment his services were used by the interior decorating department of a big store, but without Mrs Maugham's direction the crackled finish he produced on painted furniture became banal and commercialized.

In October 1939 Mrs Maugham sold the stock of her shop in Paradise Walk to Fortnum and Mason and went to Canada.

OTHER INFLUENTIAL DECORATORS

A celebrated figure between the wars, Lady Colefax, working under the name of Sybil Colefax, was reputed to have financed her ambitions as a political hostess by her talents as an interior decorator. Harold Nicolson records in his diary that Lady Colefax "tells me that she has made £2000 last year by her own sole efforts" —a considerable sum of money in 1931. No more nor less original than the majority of her semi-professional colleagues, she worked in an idiom of a blend of modern and antique, creating rooms with an atmosphere of expensive prettiness but which on closer examination were basically variations on the same theme. Characteristic elements were spotted, striped and check fabrics, and glazed chintz for cushions and curtains.

Herman Schrijver's interiors combined antique and modern furniture to achieve an effect of luxurious comfort. Discreet and without any strivings after theatrical effects, this type of decoration was, in fact, preponderant and strictly speaking has more claim than any other to the term International Style. With minor variations this highly expert blending of new and old was created by the best—and least publicized

Above: Bedroom decorated by Alistair Maynard in 1938—an opulently feminine interior, modern but with period references. The buttoned and quilted satin, and the use of mirrors and mirror-glass, create an effect of luxury which is close to excess and, at the same time, has the impersonality of a hotel bedroom.

Left: Sitting room decorated by Herman Schrijver for Dame Marie Tempest, in celadon green with curtains of red with a yellow and green flower design, before 1938.

Right: Lady Mendl, in an embroidered jacket by Schiaparelli, photographed by Cecil Beaton beside an opulent blackamoor. An interior designed by her in the baroque fashion is shown on page 197.

—decorators in England, France and the United States during the thirties. It still has many adherents.

Alistair Maynard had a career in the British Army culminating in his appointment as ADC to the Governor of Bengal. In 1935 he opened a decorating and furnishing business in Grosvenor Street, London, and through his contacts was able to create many schemes for maharajahs' palaces in India and for their houses in London. Furniture to his designs was made by the workshops of Betty Joel Ltd.

Lady Mendl, formerly Elsie de Wolfe, who had declared in an interview reported in *The Studio* in 1933, "I don't consider a room complete until it has a fine parquet floor and a painted ceiling," was credited with the revival of baroque about 1937, but a number of decorators, including Serge Roche, had already been experimenting in this idiom for some years.

FRANCE

EMILE-JACQUES RUHLMANN

The sudden death of Emile-Jacques Ruhlmann in November 1933 robbed French craftsmanship of one of its finest exponents and one worthy of comparison with Weisweiler, Reisener or Jacob. The fifty-four-year-old doyen of decorators was at the height of his powers and still enjoying the reputation which had been anticipated in 1913 at the time of his first exhibition at the Salon d'Automne and confirmed in 1919 when, in collaboration with Laurent, he opened in business. Throughout the twenties the name of Ruhlmann was synonymous with a luxurious combination of fine design, rare materials and consummate craftsmanship. The most precious veneers, exquisitely applied, were enhanced by ivory, tortoiseshell, shagreen or the finest leather; these precious pieces of furniture were themselves displayed against backgrounds of silk, velvet, satin, damask or leather. His exhibit at the Paris 1925 Exhibition was much discussed as being a summing-up of the best of the current style, as Bing's Maison de L'Art Nouveau had been in 1900. He had his imitators as any great innovator has, but nobody came within measuring distance of his taste, style and elegance. Ruhlmann's clientele was

extremely rich and he was totally uninterested in creating furniture and decors for any but the extremely rich—for him there was only the best in materials and craftsmanship. No less than sixteen draughtsmen were in his studio engaged in translating his sketches into working drawings. He employed only the most skilled workmen and retained their services by paying more than the usual rates—in return he expected them to be at the top of their form all their working hours.

The Depression made little difference to Ruhlmann's career. His work was constantly in demand by private clients as well as the French government which engaged him to design for their embassies—which, like the luxury liners, they regarded as showcases for the best in French art and craftsmanship. One of the last commissions he executed was the dining room in the French embassy in Tokyo, the long dining table showing the tendency toward the monumental which was characteristic of Ruhlmann's later works. During the previous year he had exhibited his latest models in conjunction with works of art of the seventeenth and eighteenth centuries to stress the classical quality of his furniture—a chromium and marble console supported a bust by Caffieri while an ebony cabinet was placed below a portrait by Largillière.

In the same year he created a decor for the theatre—possibly his only essay in this branch of decorative art. The play *Christine* by Paul Geraldy was presented at the Comédie Française in December 1932 and each act showed different aspects of the same room, which was represented by a curtain extending around the stage and looped up at different places to indicate various entrances or windows. To set off his furniture Ruhlmann insisted upon this curtain being

The redecoration in the Modernist style of the palace of the Maharajah of Indore was carried out under the direction of the German architect Eckhart Muthesius in 1930–33, with the collaboration of a number of leading designers, including Emile-Jacques Ruhlmann, Louis Sognot, Eileen Gray, René Herbst, Le Corbusier and Da Silva Bruhns. In the study (*above right*), the desk, chairs, sofa and cabinets, of macassar ebony with chromium-plated metal details, were by Ruhlmann, and the carpet by Da Silva Bruhns. A portrait of the Maharajah hangs in the entrance hall (*right*).

of a certain shade of grey-beige and hundreds of yards of material were specially woven, dyed and presented to the production by Paul Rodier (for whom Ruhlmann had in 1931 decorated a library in oak panelling with macassar ebony furniture covered in tobacco-coloured velvet). In collaboration with Reco Capey, Ruhlmann designed the interior of premises in Old

Entrance doors for Yardley, designed in gilt bronze by the company's artistic designer and consultant, Reco Capey, in 1932. Capey designed compacts and bottles for the cosmetics firm, and collaborated with Emile-Jacques Ruhlmann on a complete redecoration scheme for Yardley's offices and showrooms.

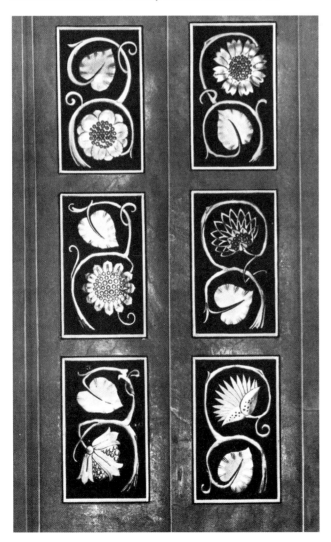

Bond Street for Yardley, the scent manufacturers. This scheme was replaced after the war but a number of pieces of the furniture bearing witness to the collaboration survived and were presented by Yardley to Brighton Museum to mark the two-hundredth anniversary of the firm.

In November 1934 Mme Ruhlmann organized a retrospective exhibition of her late husband's work at the Pavillon de Marsan. With no little difficulty she succeeded in gathering together examples of the most celebrated models he had created during the past twenty-five years, from the light, delicately inlaid and gracefully curved pieces of the early twenties to the last essays in the combination of chromium-plated steel, glass and wood.

JEAN-MICHEL FRANK

Jean-Michel Frank was a designer whose highly individual approach to decoration and furniture found admirers on both sides of the Atlantic. His career had started in the early twenties and his interiors had much in common with the most sophisticated classical rooms of Japan. To an uninitiated eye they might appear featureless—there is an apocryphal story that the bailiffs visited a financially embarrassed lady, gazed despondently at the decorations by Frank and departed remarking that there was no point in their remaining, as obviously everything had been removed by bailiffs who had arrived earlier. But to a discerning eye the virtues of the decorations were apparent, the delicate proportions of the furniture, the exquisite craftsmanship and above all the subtle varieties of the surfaces. Ivory, lacquer, vellum, shagreen, suede, calfskin, morocco, straw—these were among the favourite materials used by Frank to clothe and ornament the chaste lines of his furniture uncluttered by mouldings or carved motifs. Of all the woods his preference was for oak, preferably unstained and treated to make the grain stand out in relief. The rich dark markings of macassar favoured by Ruhlmann or the blond insipidity of sycamore used by so many of his contemporaries had no appeal for him. Another point of resemblance with Japanese rooms was the flexibility of arrangement of the furniture—he rarely included a commode or cabinet large enough to

simplicity and a dining room with panels by Christian Bérard. In 1935 he designed showrooms for the dressmakers Lelong and Schiaparelli—he had decorated the latter's apartment in a style which had made her rival Chanel "shudder as though she had passed a graveyard", as Schiaparelli gleefully records in her autobiography *Shocking Life*.

In the United States Frank executed decorations for the Nelson Rockefeller apartment in New York and for the Templeton Crocker house in San Francisco, where he installed lacquered panels by Jean Dunand. Individual pieces of furniture designed in collaboration with Rodocanacchi and lamps designed for him by the sculptor Diego Giacometti embellished houses on both sides of the Atlantic. A collaboration between Diego Giacometti and his brother Alberto was responsible for a number of plaster and bronze lamps, decorative vases, tables and chairs commissioned and sold by Jean-Michel Frank.

In 1939 Frank abandoned his usual subtle variations on the theme of white and beige and in a scheme

Above: Furnishings by Jean-Michel Frank: vellum-covered tables, a strip-veneered folding screen and a rough rock crystal block mounted as a lamp.

dominate the room or monopolize one position around which all the other pieces had to adopt fixed positions.

Frank's work was to be found in Paris, South America, New York and San Francisco. In 1931 he decorated a houseboat for the Vicomte de Noailles, in white with white-lacquered furniture of deceptive

Below: Plaster table lamp by Giacometti for Jean-Michel Frank: the light is concealed in the central vase so that the lamp, placed on a side table, illuminates a picture on the wall above. The design is reminiscent of the elaborately carved alabaster ornaments found in the tomb of Tutankhamun.

for a ballroom for Baron de Roland de l'Epée indulged in a harmony of the confectionery colours favoured by Christian Bérard whose talents had been equivocally lauded in an article in *Art Direction* as "a genius for colour, a sense of arrangement, effeminate taste, morbid romanticism and perversity". In this room each wall was painted a different colour, rose, blue, yellow and green, with small settees upholstered in the same shades. Three of these were copies of Second Empire models while the fourth was that made from a design by Salvador Dali in the shape of Mae West's lips. These were set off by a dark red carpet and in two corners of the room were curved pavilions draped with red vel-

vet curtains and frames in white plaster barley-sugar columns. A screen painted by de Pisis completed the decor which was reminiscent of Bérard's decor for the ballet *Cotillon* with its arrangement of a series of boxes with red curtains against walls of white *faux marbre*.

PAUL RUAUD

The juxtaposition of primitive African sculpture and ancient Egyptian art in an extremely modern setting was employed by Suzanne Talbot in her drawing room in Paris and photographs of this striking decor were shown in *L'Illustration* in 1933. The scheme, by Paul Ruaud, incorporated furniture by Eileen Gray and

Above: Suzanne Talbot's drawing room, decorated by Paul Ruaud, with the tubular steel "Bibendum" armchairs designed by Eileen Gray in 1926–29. The sliding doors on the left are of dark blue glass.

Left: The Paris drawing room of Suzanne Talbot (Mme Mathieu Lévy), decorated by Paul Ruaud in the early 1930s with furniture by Eileen Gray, including lacquered pieces created by her ten years earlier for the same apartment. The walls are white, and the floor and door panels are of satinized glass.

white versions of the "brick" screens created some ten years earlier by Miss Gray in black lacquer. This room, if reconstructed today, nearly sixty years later, would have as contemporary an air as any to be found in current decorating magazines and would not, unlike many of the rooms of the early thirties, appear in the

least dated. The floor, the doors and some folding screens were covered in dull silver glass, contrasting with the white satin-finished cellulose paint on the walls. The upholstery of the steel chairs by Eileen Gray was in white leather and the bold stripes of zebra skins enlivened the floors and a divan. Two carved wood spirit stools from the Gold Coast and a number of Egyptian funerary vases contributed to the timeless atmosphere.

ANDRÉ ARBUS

In 1931 André Arbus was the director of L'Epoque, working somewhat in the tradition of Ruhlmann but lacking the restraint and sobriety which characterized the latter's work. While more influenced by the past than by contemporary themes, Arbus's work was criticized on the grounds that the sinuous, calligraphic

lines of his furniture were not always happily conceived, his chairs in particular often giving a somewhat precarious sense of balance. In the later thirties he adopted the more serenely classical style of the late eighteenth century and in some cases, particularly in some work he did in the theatre, he appears to have been influenced by the designs of Ledoux. He created a series of rooms for the Paris Exhibition in 1937.

EUGÈNE PRINTZ

Printz was recognized as one of France's leading *ébénistes* and *ensembliers* of the thirties, developing a highly personal idiom, working with palmwood, incorporating laquer and metalwork by Jean Dunand and developing his own idiosyncratic forms for the metal supports to his pieces. Amongst his best-known and most characteristic schemes were rooms deco-

Above: Bedroom decorated by Eugène Printz for the Princesse de la Tour d'Auvergne, 1930.

Left: Cabinet by Eugène Printz of green lacquered wood, lined in sycamore with patinated metal feet and mounts. This piece of furniture is of the finest craftsmanship, combining lacquer, metal and glass in an unconventional design that owes nothing to traditional sources.

Far left: Design for a living room of a house on the Ile de France, Paris, by André Arbus, shown at the Paris 1937 Exhibition.

rated for the Princesse de la Tour d'Auvergne in 1930. The bedroom, exhibited at the 1930 Salon des Artistes-Décorateurs, drew from Guillaume Janneau the comment that such a "remarkable combination . . . prompts us to query whether it is a drawing room or a boudoir. The pieces are designed in modern, rational forms: rare woods ingeniously allied with metal supports, lids that slide, tip or pivot, subtle colouring: the imagination of a *modiste* with the precision of an engineer."

Such an exhibit exemplified the custom, unknown in England, of French decorators allowing the general public to view either the actual scheme or a reproduction of work commissioned by distinguished patrons.

4
ART AND INDUSTRY

ENGLAND

esign in Modern Life by John Gloag was one of a number of books published in the early thirties at the height of the Depression, the effects of which upon the domestic and the export trade provided an opportunity for the advocates of a closer relationship between art and industry. More and more influential voices were to be heard preaching the doctrine that only by an increased standard of design could business improve and as the financial state of the country worsened more people were inclined to listen and to act upon their advice.

In view of the admiration for the exhibits in the Swedish Exhibition of 1930 the editor of *The Architectural Review* expressed what in his opinion were the reasons for the higher quality of decorative art in Sweden as compared to England. Apart from the benefit of having been neutral during the First World War with the advantages of being able to continue traditions of craftsmanship uninterrupted, there was a far closer degree of cooperation between Swedish designers and manufacturers than had ever been possible in England. There was also, he commented,

Left: Mass-produced plywood chairs with painted seats in the Sanatorium at Paimio, Finland, designed by Alvar Aalto in 1929–33.

the added benefit for the Swedes of having a royal family actively interested in the arts. The King and his brothers Carl and Oscar were all actively interested in theatre; another brother, Eugen, was a painter of considerable talent; the Crown Prince was an archaeologist of repute, while Prince Sigvard designed silverware which was made by Georg Jensen. It was felt that in comparison the English royal family made a poor showing, their patronage being confined to the opening of occasional exhibitions. However, the Prince of Wales lent his support and in several speeches stated bluntly that "if British trade is to hold its own in the markets of the world it must do more than maintain the technical excellence in which it has so long enjoyed leadership: it must raise the standard of design in its products, for in design it is outstripped by other countries." Such an opinion, even coming from one who on his own admission was far from being an authority on the arts, carried weight if only because of his personal popularity.

Whether it was the result of the Prince of Wales's influence or not, the practical step was taken by the government of forming a committee under the chairmanship of Lord Gorell to deal with art in industry. Their findings and recommendations were published in 1932 in what came to be generally known as the Gorell Report. Among the numerous suggestions made were that special buildings should be provided for exhibitions of industrial art in London and the provinces, each exhibition to last for at least six weeks with a permanent show of the best products of contemporary design, that there should be travelling exhibitions in both Britain and in foreign countries and—here followed the most difficult idea to implement—that there should be an improvement in the status of industrial artists, together with an active encouragement of manufacturers to use first-rate designers. Finally it was stressed that there should be better art education and research into methods and needs of industry in so far as design was concerned.

The Gorell Report had a definite response from the Bourneville organization founded by the Cadbury family. In 1932 this took the form of an offer of £1000 a year for artists for designs suitable for use on chocolate boxes, lack of experience in the industry being of no importance. The standard of packaging of medium-priced confectionery had been for years on the lowest level of appeal, with a stress on white Persian kittens or lush herbaceous borders, while the more expensive hand-made chocolates were packaged in satin boxes hand-painted with ladies in crinolines or sprays of roses. ''Chocolate-box prettiness'' had come to denote over-sweet charm. In order to attract a more serious type of design a competition was announced with a prize of 100 guineas, in addition to the prizes (already offered prior to the Gorell Report) awarded each year in the annual Competitions of Industrial Design organized by the Royal Society of Arts. Several hundred entries were received and a considerable number sub-

sequently purchased. Furthermore, a prestige range of boxes was planned and a number of well-known painters were invited to submit designs. They were given a free hand and of those invited only two were rejected as being unsuitable, the remaining eleven, after being exhibited at the Leicester Galleries, being reproduced and making their appearance in the confectioners' windows in 1934. The majority of the artists invited to participate were conventional in their approach to the problems involved, but two among them were still regarded in more academic circles as *avant-garde*. Mark Gertler's contribution was a still life of fruit and flowers, colourful but betraying the waning powers of a painter succumbing to ill-health and melancholia—he committed suicide in 1939. The ''Exotic'' box with a spiritless tropical view framed by curtains bore the surprising name of C. R. W. Nevinson, the solitary English Futurist and recorder of the devastation of the First World War but, like Gertler, of declining power during the thirties. Others were by Arthur Watts, the humorous artist; Dame Laura Knight—two contributions, a circus scene and a forcefully drawn portrait of a ballerina; Philip Connard, a decorative painter who had executed murals in Windsor Castle; George Sheringham, the talented theatrical designer; Edmund Dulac, illustrator of many fairy stories; Arthur Rackham, and Dod Proctor and her husband Ernest.

Silver box by Harold Stabler, 1932.

The constant propaganda similarly influenced the makers of Foley pottery and the directors of the Royal Staffordshire Pottery to cooperate in a presentation of pottery and glassware designed by a number of leading artists—Duncan Grant, Vanessa Bell, Dame Laura Knight, Graham Sutherland, Barbara Hepworth, Mary Crofts (Dame Laura's sister), Paul Nash, Ben Nicholson, Frank Brangwyn, John Armstrong, Dod Proctor and Albert Rutherston—who were given a free hand with no restrictions. Any adjustments necessary for technical reasons or due to lack of practical experience on the part of the designers were made only after consultation with the designer concerned. The actual painting of these designs on the ware was entrusted to Clarice Cliff, creator of the "Bizarre" designs for A. J. Wilkinson Ltd, or her assistants. After two years' work the finished results were shown in 1934 in an exhibition of "Modern Ware for the Table". In an opening speech Sir William Rothenstein commented that since Flaxman's work for Josiah Wedgwood no British artist of any standing had been asked to design ceramics. One reason for this long separation between artist and manufacturer was of course the circumstances that not since the days of Flaxman

Above left: Ceramic plate manufactured by Arthur J. Wilkinson & Co of Burslem, Staffordshire, with decoration by John Armstrong, 1934.

Above: Engraved glass vase designed by Graham Sutherland and made by Stuart and Sons, 1934.

Below: Ceramic mug manufactured by Josiah Wedgwood & Sons of Etruria, Staffordshire, with decoration by Eric Ravilious, 1936.

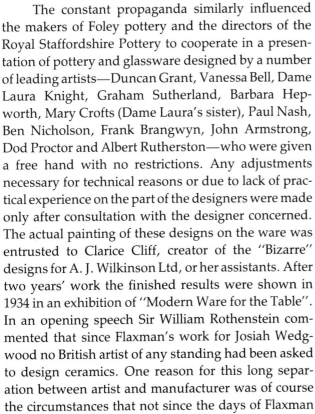

Carpet designed by Ronald Grierson in about 1935.

had there been conditions of financial and industrial depression severe enough to bring together the fine and applied arts from necessity on both sides. A critical comment in *The Studio* gives a clue to another possible reason: "It must be admitted regretfully that some of the designs were quite unsuited to the purpose for which they were intended."

The article did continue on a more optimistic note, "the Exhibition was of great importance as it marked the inauguration of a policy which will no doubt be extensively followed." But in general the constant exhortations to manufacturers to improve the standards of design which came from various official and unofficial bodies, and the repetition of the slogan "Design or decline—plan or perish" by the Prince of Wales in his speeches, either fell on deaf ears or, if the members of a particular industry were feeling the effects of the general depression, posed problems which seemed insuperable. It was all very well to emphasize the importance of design, but the real

question was where could the manufacturers find the designers capable of creating work original and arresting enough to tempt new customers at home and abroad. Designers of little or no talent could assemble "period" motifs with not much effort provided they had sufficient technical knowledge, but the new wave of "Modernism" was another matter.

"Manufacturers and dealers, snuffing the prevailing wind, call up their hack designers and command them to 'Jazz things up a bit'," wrote Paul Nash in *Room and Book* and in many cases this jazzing-up process consisted of pirating designs from French pattern books—for there were no English equivalents from which they could adapt examples. Several examples can be found in *A Survey of British Industrial Arts*. The hammered iron grilles and the bronze balustrades carried out by Gardiner and Sons for the Forum Cinema, Bath, were obviously inspired by examples of the work of Edgar Brandt and Raymond Subes in *La Ferronerie Moderne*—a volume issued to commemorate the wrought iron and metal work in the Paris 1925 Exhibition. The conventionalized flower forms, the use of spirals and the flat bands twisted to look like crumpled ribbon are direct copies from the French prototypes and similarly a carpet by John Crossley and Sons illustrated in the same book is a coarsened ver-

sion of one by Da Silva Bruhns. Elsewhere one can find many examples of fabrics and wallpapers adapted from designs by Edouard Bénédictus, Mme de Andrada and other French designers whose work appeared (reproduced in colour by the *pochoir* process) in French pattern books, despite warnings against breach of copyright. That their work would be pirated must have occurred to the artists and to the publishers but the pity is that it was usually done with such insensitivity and in such a way as to destroy all the original style and elegance.

Oak sideboard manufactured and retailed by Heal & Son, London.

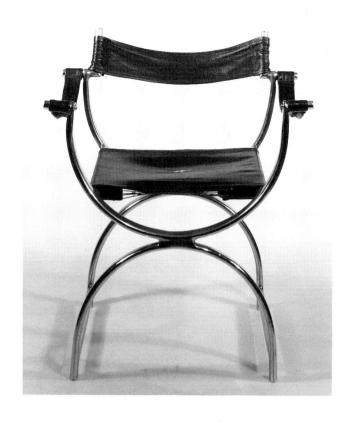

Curtis Moffat, the American photographer who had in 1929 opened a gallery in Fitzroy Square and one of the few disciples of Modernism active in England, played an important role in the British exhibit at the international exhibition at Monza in 1930. *The Studio* had proudly announced in the issue of July 1929 that the magazine had been entrusted by the Italian government with the task of organizing the British section. This was at a time when Mussolini was still generally regarded in a favourable light and the editorial staff of *The Studio* were anxious to introduce British manufacturers and their wares "to a great and friendly nation, keenly interested in British productions, an importing and exporting country which, under the new regime, has awakened to an unexampled vigour and the prospect of brilliant developments in every sphere." On the surface the British section appeared to have made a successful showing with exhibits by

Above: Armchair designed by Sir Ambrose Heal in oval-sectioned chromium-plated steel and leather, presented at the British Art in Industry Exhibition, 1935.

Left: Cocktail cabinet designed by J. C. Pritchard, shown at the Monza Exhibition of 1930, an experimental effort to use metal-covered "Plymax" for furniture. A somewhat unfortunate resemblance to a kitchen stove seems to have inhibited any further attempts in this direction. Plymax was used architecturally, however, usually for interior doors.

Right: Plywood armchair designed by Gerald Summers and manufactured by Makers of Simple Furniture in about 1934. The chair is cut and bent from a single rectangular sheet of plywood.

the Rowley Gallery, Edinburgh Weavers, Doulton and Gordon Russell as well as Curtis Moffat; and Mussolini congratulated the organizers after being shown round. Cook's tours were organized to bring visitors from England and it was agreed that the general standard of design was an improvement on the British exhibit at the Paris 1925 Exhibition. But an acid note creeps in to the comments by the editor of *The Studio* and suggests that difficulties had been encountered in finding an adequate selection. The cooperation between manufacturers and artists common on the Continent was almost unknown in England: it was found, for example, that there were commercial printers in Paris who had fifty artists on their staff, whereas in England it was unusual to find even one. Several pages of photographs of the exhibits were featured in *The Studio* but even the most chauvinistic critic could not have described them as being particularly impressive, and this mediocre showing undoubtedly gave an impetus to efforts to bring about a closer cooperation between art and industry—efforts which were to culminate in the Royal Academy Exhibition of 1935.

For several seasons, since the beginning of the decade, the Royal Academy, under the presidency of Sir William Llewellyn, had organized important winter exhibitions of the arts of the past or of other countries. Those of the arts of Persia and of China proved particularly successful, the former revealing aspects of the artistic tradition of the Middle East which had never been shown to the general public before, while the latter, which included the greater part of the Eumorphopoulos collection, displayed a series of masterpieces of Chinese art of all periods which confirmed the long-held interest of the English in the culture of that country. This series of historical exhibitions was interrupted in 1935 when "British Art in Industry" was chosen as the theme for the winter show. Organized under the joint auspices of the Royal Academy and the Royal Society of Arts the published theme of the exhibition had a familiar ring: "to impress upon the public the importance of good design in articles of everyday use; to show not only to our own people but also to other nations that British manufacturers in cooperation with British artists are capable of

producing in all branches of industry articles which combine artistic form with utility and sound workmanship; to encourage British artists to give to industry the benefit of their talents and training so that the objects with which we are surrounded in our daily lives may have an appearance which is not only attractive but is based on genuinely artistic principles."

A great deal was written on the subject of art in industry about the time of the Burlington House Exhibition and some of the arguments put forward were optimistic in the extreme. John Milne, the chairman of The Medici Society, advanced the view that "in so far as greater beauty in his products is achieved by the manufacturer when his wares are brought among a growing public, joy and happiness will be spread in wider and wider circles. At the same time there will take place an improvement in the average level of taste. This will in its turn lead to a demand for further improvements in all goods and wares. Thus the small beginnings of good taste and enthusiasm for beauty introduced by the more progressive manufacturers and salesmen will have the effect of leavening the whole process of production and distribution and will tend towards the diffusion of greater happiness among the people through a wider appreciation of beauty."

Such idealism inevitably drew a cynical reaction, and admirable as the aims of the organizers may have been, they were no more successful in convincing the public, artists or manufacturers than those of previous exhibitions. The annual Ideal Homes Exhibition organized by the *Daily Mail* provided a popular and spectacular opportunity for manufacturers to show their latest products to the general public but while every care was taken by the sponsor to present a lively, entertaining display, the fact remains that the exhibition was a commercial venture and any firm able to afford the hiring of a stand was allowed to exhibit, no matter how low the standard of design of the furniture, china or fancy goods. To avoid this, the organizers of the 1935 Exhibition decided that merit alone would be the deciding factor for inclusion. The unavoidable result was hostility on the part of those firms whose work had been rejected, who were naturally disinclined to learn any lessons from it. And the efforts

Boxes by Reco Capey made of wood with carved finials, exhibited at the British Art in Industry Exhibition of 1935. The finial in the shape of a rabbit on the right was the first use of Perspex as a decorative material, the result of an experiment by Capey, using a sample block sent to him by the manufacturers.

of the organizers were received with caustic comments from the popular newspapers and from journals more directly connected with the arts and design. They could draw small comfort from the comment in *The Studio* that "the exhibition marks a great step forward and will lead on to further advances", while *Reynolds' Illustrated News* was describing it as "an attempt to humbug the public" and Anthony Blunt in the *Spectator* was informing his readers that "it comprised the vulgarity of Tottenham Court Road, the sham modernity of Wigmore Street, the expensiveness of Bond Street", and that it was "a shock to find that almost every quality which disfigured industrial objects of the nineteenth century was here". The decorative setting for the exhibition, widely publicized as having cost £20,000, a considerable sum of money in the thirties, and as having required the services of thirty-one experts, came in for its share of adverse comment. "Eastern bazaars", wrote a critic in *The Times*, "about which it would have been more appropriate to boast if only £500 had been spent." The contribution of one of the thirty-one experts, Rex Whistler, whose reputation as a decorative artist was rapidly growing, was

dismissed as "an icing-sugar fantasy" while that of his colleagues was as severely castigated. Three of the exhibits in particular seem to have aroused the hostility of the critics. Oliver Hill's garden dining room with its engraved marble walls, marble floor and "marble-stuc" chairs was described as "a piece of heartless and extravagant snobbery"—a contrast to the praise which had met a rather similar dining room with engraved marble walls designed by René Lalique for the Paris Exhibition ten years before. An eccentrically shaped bed on a revolving circular platform designed by Betty Joel earned general condemnation as "a dislocated hip-bath" while Robert Lutyens's breakfast table consisting of a circular plate-glass top suspended from the ceiling by three metal rods was greeted with a storm of abuse.

The critics seem to have taken exception to these three exhibits in particular as typifying a tendency on the part of the organizers to include the expensive and the fantastic for, in their view, "industry should imply mass production", a conception which certainly could not be said to include marble walls, revolving beds or hanging tables. For the organizers it must be pointed

Left: Writing desk designed by Alistair Maynard and manufactured by Betty Joel Ltd in 1934; shown at the British Art in Industry Exhibition in 1935. Made of sycamore with a parchment top and ivory handles, it is an example of the veering away from stark functionalism towards a more decorative idiom, a tendency that characterized many of the exhibits and that aroused sharp criticism in the case of the more extreme examples. Fluting, both concave and convex, was used by a number of designers as a comparatively economical means of breaking up plain surfaces.

Below left: David Joel in his office, 1935.

Below: Living room designed by Betty Joel in the early 1930s. The warm tones of the pine-panelled walls contrast with the natural ivory colour of the sycamore furniture, and are set off by the Betty Joel rug.

out that the previous exhibitions had been financially rewarding in spite of the costs of transporting and insuring the precious objects and paintings and the attendance figures had increased with each show. They realized that the public would not flock with equal enthusiasm to a display of mass-produced articles however well designed—the practical lily had to be gilded with a certain amount of novelty to attract publicity and to give the exhibition a popular appeal. But harsh as the critical comments were—and they were not balanced by praise—there was some justification for them. A writer in *The Architectural Review* commented on the pottery, porcelain and glass that "the pottery section shows a complete lack of life;

there has been no improvement on the traditional forms which originated in the eighteenth century and perhaps these forms cannot be improved upon—why then lower the quality of the design by excluding them from the exhibition? . . . the decoration is timid and ineffectual"; with reference to glass the writer continues, "everywhere timidity, lack of inspiration, refusal to let the material have its way", ending with the faint praise that "there is a commendable lack of cut glass of the prickly variety". One of the organizing committee, H. S. Goodhart-Rendel, the vice-president of the Royal Institute of British Architects, gave a clue when he wrote that the idea before the selecting committee could be summarized as "no copies and no stunts". The exclusion of copies of past styles had been one of the rules of the Paris Exhibition of 1925. There was no clear definition of "stunts" and some rectangular dinner plates in the pottery section were included simply because of "their popularity in the market". The next year the Royal Academy reverted to a historical exhibition for its winter season, though the annual exhibition of contemporary painting remained one of the highlights of the summer season.

The two associations which could have been influential in persuading or even forcing manufacturers to improve their standards of design were, in the opinion of John Gloag, so ineffectual as to be negligible. Writing in 1934, when the need for an improvement in the quality of design in British goods for export was as pressing as ever, he gives his reasons in the opening chapter of *Industrial Art Explained*. The Royal Society of Arts with a history going back to 1754 was founded for "The Encouragement of the Arts, Manufactures and Commerce of the Country" with rewards for inventions and improvements in industry, applied science and art, agriculture, chemistry and engineering. A later development was the inauguration of a Fund for the Preservation of Ancient Cottages. Though the RSA was the first body to identify the existence of industrial art, "it suffers from a diversity of intention . . . it cannot encourage 'the Arts, Manufactures and Commerce of the Country' unless it is prepared to lead industry." "The Design and Industries Association", Gloag declared, "could never have been formed in a really civilized country

because no civilized country would have permitted industry to get into a condition in which its products were so fantastically inept that many manufacturers had to be reminded that fitness for purpose was a basic principle of design in everything." Founded in 1915, any progress it might have made was crippled for lack of funds, though it had some small influence through propaganda for the doctrine of fitness for purpose.

The basic tenets of fitness for purpose were, of course, perfectly sensible. Obviously a teapot, for instance, should pour without dribbling, hold the heat of its contents and be easy to clean (although, incidentally, some of the square teapots designed in the new spirit failed to do any of these things), and so on with all objects made for a functional purpose. But the propaganda tended to harp too much upon industry, to mention too often the word machine: in the public mind associations were aroused with the film *Metropolis* with its alarming (at the time) world of machinery and servant human robots, or with the much-publicized phrase of Le Corbusier, "a home is a machine for living in", and other slogans connected with design, particularly with architectural design, which were circulated "to comfort bright young people who wanted to be aesthetically modish without the fatigue of thinking". The logical argument that because an article was made by a machine it should not look as though it had been made by hand became slanted to the view that it should look like a machine. As Gloag pointed out, "mechanical forms are used as patterns for textiles and wallpapers: they provide inspiration for the mechanistic baroque style of a decoration but they do not represent a real industrial contribution to design." The reformers and advocates of fitness for purpose condemned the mass-produced ornament applied during the nineteenth century after the Industrial Revolution and were resistant to the fact that, however wrong it may have been in theory, in practice much of it had great charm. Unhappily they had no substitute to offer. Simple unadorned geometrical shapes, whether in furniture or pottery, had a limited appeal for the English buying public which, in the main, dearly loved a nice pink rose. Patriotism itself had to be used as a selling point, for instance in the case of the 1931 advertisement by Best and Lloyd, whose Modernistic table lamp was captioned "Modern—but English". It is ironic that at the time when the purists were condemning Victorian designers as being the original culprits for the poor standards of design current in 1930, fashion was already turning its attention to Victoriana. Curtis Moffat denounced the reconstruction of the Victorian room as "an amusing exercise in horror" in 1931. In the same year an article in *Vogue* was entitled "The Victorian Age Returns"—and within a few years many of Curtis Moffat's clients were to be enthusiastically collecting buttoned furniture, papier-mâché and shell flowers under glass shades.

A factory scene from the "machine age" film, *Metropolis*, directed by Fritz Lang, 1926.

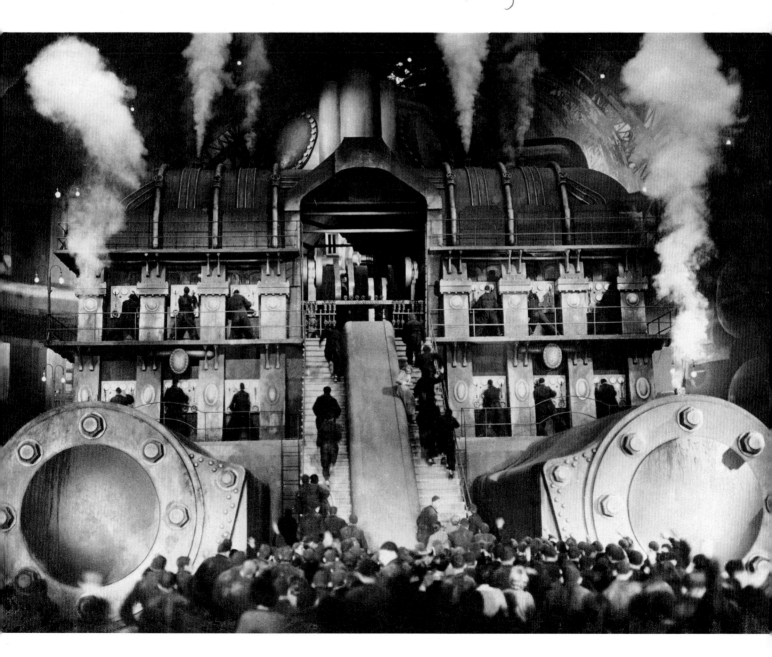

Left: Metal table lamp, early 1930s: the striving after novelty of such self-consciously geometric forms was a corollary of the new Modernism.

Below: "Fate", a ceramic head made by Doulton & Co from a model created by Richard Garbe, 1934.

Right: Decorative painted wood panel made and sold by the Rowley Gallery, London, about 1930.

Another fact that the enthusiasts for fitness for purpose tended to forget is that an original piece of design, however theoretically functional that design may be, is still a reflection in some way or another of the time in which it was made and consequently governed by the laws of fashion. This does not apply to objects the design of which is the result of decades or even hundreds of years of use, where the form and design have been evolved by constant modifications or imperceptible alterations. Anything from a piece of furniture to an egg-cup fashioned according to the theories of functional design in, say, 1932 will look old-fashioned a few years later, no matter how chaste the form or how little ornamented. It was this factor that made many people hesitate to favour Modernism to any great extent—apart from the fact that such a step would entail their getting rid of possessions which were likely to interfere with the over-all func-

longer applied any more than it did to Queen Anne or Chippendale furniture. By collecting Victoriana one demonstrated an awareness of trends without running the risk of finding oneself living in *démodé* surroundings—the Victoriana could only become more antique and consequently respectable with time.

THE UNITED STATES

Meanwhile in America the Metropolitan Museum of Art, New York, was indefatigable in its efforts to further a *rapprochement* between fine and industrial art, from its first Exhibition of Industrial Art in 1917 when most, if not all, of the exhibits were designed with objects in the museum collection as inspiration. For the next eight years the same principle was followed but in 1924 it was noted that there were a small number of pieces which owed nothing to historical references and in 1925 the museum purchased a selection of the best exhibits from the Paris 1925 Exhibition. In 1927 the display was limited to American products designed and made by American residents while two years later the exhibits were custom-made contemporary pieces. Possibly as a result of the Depression, from 1930 the exhibition consisted entirely of artefacts obtainable on the market and in 1934, as a result of the cooperation of nineteen leading architects and designers, the strictly contemporary designs on exhibit proved so popular that no less than 139,000 people attended the exhibition.

tional look. Consequently when Regency and, at a later date, Victorian furniture and ornaments emerged from the no-man's-land of unfashionableness and were once more allowed to become objects for admiration—even if that admiration had a flavour of amused patronage—they were acclaimed because the question of their being dated or old-fashioned no

5

INTERIOR FURNISHINGS

STEEL FURNITURE

Possibly the most characteristic feature of Modernist interiors in the early thirties was the use of chromium-plated tubular steel furniture and the main source in England was Practical Equipment Limited, more generally known as PEL. This firm was started from the chance placing in the newly decorated Strand Palace Hotel of two steel chairs of Continental origin by the hotel's designer Oliver Bernard. These attracted the attention of one of

the directors of Tube Investments Ltd, who saw the possibilities of extending the activities of his firm in the field of prestige products. Bernard was placed under contract as a consultant designer between 1931 and 1932 and the PEL shop in Henrietta Place attracted an affluent and fashionable clientele by the novelty of the gleaming chromium-plated furniture—which nearly

Left: Bar in the Queen's Hotel, Leeds, designed by Curtis Green in 1937. The tubular steel furniture dates from the early 1930s and was made by PEL: it includes ''BS5'' stools, ''M60'' tables and ''SP4'' armchairs.

Below: Metal and glass sideboard by Desny, early 1930s.

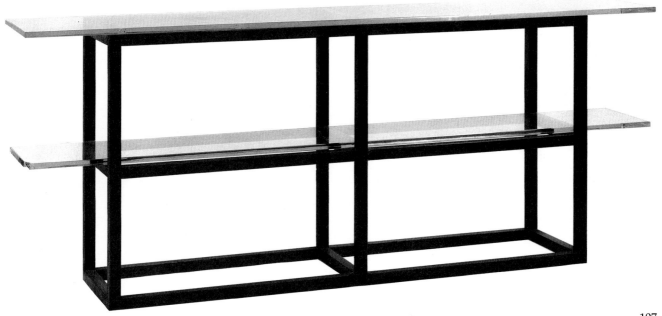

Left: Armchair designed by Louis Sognot in chromium-plated metal and leather with the back resting on two large springs, early 1930s.

Below: Aluminium chaise longue by Marcel Breuer, designed in 1932 and marketed from 1933 onwards; it won first prize in an international competition for the "best aluminium chair" sponsored by the Alliance Aluminium Compagnie of France.

Right: Interior furnished with tubular steel designs, including an armchair by Emile Guillot, and a low table and "Wassily" chair by Marcel Breuer, all probably manufactured by Thonet in the early 1930s.

outshone the sapphire shirt-buttons of a frequent visitor, the Maharajah of Alwar. At this time individual pieces of furniture in steel and plate glass were made to the requirements of clients and architects but, as the technical processes improved, more and more utilitarian furniture for offices and hotels was manufactured. Among the first clients for stacking chairs was the BBC; barstools, luggage stands and traystands were made for the Savoy Hotel and Claridges. The field became ever wider with equipment for hospitals and canteens until the luxury pieces gradually came to be discontinued, partly because of a change of fashion but mainly because it was no longer practical to make them. The cantilever chairs were not cheap by the standards of the early 1930s, costing £6—though the leather covering could be dyed any shade to the client's specifications. Cox and Company, a rival firm founded soon after PEL and later incorporated in it,

advertised chairs in 1932 at £5 5s if painted in enamel and £5 10s with a chromium finish, but it was estimated that with improved methods of mass production these prices would, by 1935, fall by half.

CHEAP MASS-PRODUCED FURNITURE

In addition to new furniture—Modernist or reproduction of Tudor or Queen Anne—designed and made for a comparatively small but prosperous section of the population, there was the numerically more common type of product intended for a cheaper market and sold through hire-purchase firms, big department stores or small furniture dealers. Of this type the greater part was still made in mock-Tudor style with grotesque melon-bulb legs and imitation curved panels of steam-pressed wood; second in popularity was a mock-Georgian style using spindly stock cabriole legs, and lastly a diluted version of Modernism.

The cheap mock-antique furniture was characterized by a glittering French-polished surface and an over-indulgence in applied ornament masking a shoddiness of materials and workmanship which, unhappily for the customer but fortunately for posterity, ensured a short life. Its flashy finish had an immediate appeal to a public with no experience of or even interest in quality.

The "designers" of the pseudo-Modernist furniture reckoned that there were two special characteristics of Modernism. One was the use of steel, the other a tendency towards asymmetry. The latter was their solution to the problem of giving some originality to a piece of furniture when fashion dictated that there should be no ornamental details. So although the Modernists advocated simplicity this "Modernist" furniture was often overloaded with asymmetrical decoration. Mirrors were made with freakish and unnecessary angles, while curtains, carpets and cushions had to be covered with stripes and spots in the manner of Picasso and Braque. Furniture was so angular and unusual that it was uncomfortable both to look at and use.

Thousands of suburban villas were happily filled by their proud owners with mock-Tudor dining room suites or Modernistic bedroom suites bought on easy terms, all guaranteed to fall to pieces before the final payment was made unless handled with extreme care. Three-piece suites of elephantine proportions, covered in jazzy moquette hostile to the touch and occupying far more space than their seating accommodation warranted, were considered an absolute necessity for any young married couple setting up a home. R. Gardner Medwin, in complaining that "each year a shameless display at the British Industries Fair reveals the decadence of our furniture industry. . . . Grotesque novelty parades as 'modern'", gave vent to a *cri de cœur* that could have found echoes in France, Germany and the United States. "Taste tends to be negative rather than bad", he continued "and if the leading manufacturers would develop a conscience,

would realize the advantage of employing skilled designers, public taste would soon be found to improve beyond measure." The manufacturers he castigates must presumably have employed some designers, whether skilled or not, but with the passing of time any trace of these anonymous hacks, together with the furniture they designed, has passed into oblivion.

David Joel in his book *The Adventure of British Furniture* has a section entitled "Chamber of Horrors", giving illustrations of cheap mass-produced furniture of the period between the wars. No source is given for the illustrations, some of which appear to have been redrawn in such a manner as to accentuate the ugliness of the furniture portrayed. Grotesque they certainly are, but it is impossible to suppress the thought that they often had—in the Modernistic examples—a gusto and energy lacking in the work of many reputable designers whose efforts to rehabilitate good taste resulted in a rather anaemic and timid anonymity. An editorial comment in *House and Garden* described English contemporary furniture as "sober and conservative", a definition calculated not to antagonize advertisers but adequate to explain why those with a taste for originality should have reverted to the Victorian or baroque styles.

WALL TREATMENTS

The natural setting for steel or other Modernist furniture was plain walls. The disadvantage of plain walls, however, especially in corridors or staircases open to the public, was that ordinary painted surfaces were liable to wear or scratching both accidental and deliberate. The appearance of a number of plastic paints marketed under various names such as "Sankmar" provided a solution. The formula varied but basically was a mixture of powdered marble or mica combined with a powdered plastic. When mixed with water the resulting paste could be brushed on the wall and treated decoratively in a number of ways, a pattern incised in semicircles or shell shapes with metal combs or textures made by stipple brushes or wet rags. When dry the composition had a rock-hard surface impervious to cracking or peeling and could be painted.

Unfortunately, in spite of an attractive surface texture when freshly applied, the drawbacks were apparent after a while. The incised patterns attracted dirt which lodged in the depressions and could only be cleaned with difficulty, and once the composition had set it was almost impossible to remove. The only way to restore the wall to a smooth finish was to replaster it entirely. It continued to be used in cinemas or similar public buildings but soon lost favour as a treatment in private houses when it was found that the incised designs could not be concealed under wallpaper when fashion veered towards more decorative treatments.

Painted or distempered walls were to be found in newer houses where the wall surface was fresh and needed no attention before the paint was applied. The improvements in the quality and range of colours in

Fabric design by Raoul Dufy, 1930.

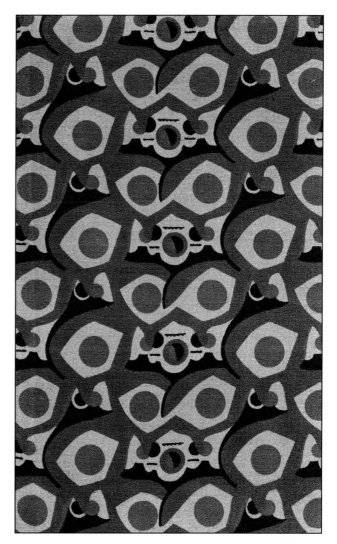

"Fugue", screen-printed linen by Paul Nash, 1936.

the brands of washable distempers which could be applied by a comparatively unskilled decorator caused some concern to the wallpaper industry.

Wallpaper itself never ceased to be used, of course, as it was one of the cheapest methods of redecoration, and there was still enough demand for plain wallpapers to justify the production of textured papers, known irreverently as "porridge", which were made in a seemingly endless range of tones of beige, cream and oatmeal in addition to extremely discreet pastel colours. These were enlivened by borders and corner motifs. The borders were between one

and three inches (2.5 to 7.5 cm) wide—rarely wider —and were usually in sad colours in geometric or floral designs of quite notable mediocrity. The corner motifs or triangular shapes were cut out and applied near the ceiling and many a room in the early thirties —and for long after—derived any character it may have had from a spray of autumn leaves in appropriate shades of orange and brown or a Modernist design in rich tones. Patterned papers were invariably geometrical in design, sometimes combined with discreetly conventionalized flowers or leaves, and these were printed in a technique which gave a curiously blurred over-all appearance. It was said that before putting a patterned paper on the market a sample wall was prepared and it was the job of an unfortunate employee to stare at this wall for days on end to detect any accidental hidden motifs which might reveal them-

Above: "The Rum Runners", design for a textile by Donald Deskey, early 1930s.

Right: Abstract design in watercolour for a textile by Donald Deskey, 1930–31.

selves, such as grimacing faces or worse. There was an apocryphal story that one firm had marketed several thousand rolls of a new paper before complaints flowed in that the pattern when applied to the wall resolved itself into unexpected motifs of astonishing eroticism. This type of paper was confined to the lower price ranges while at the other end of the scale there were the expensive damask papers of the type used in museums, art galleries and the drawing rooms of large period houses. There was so little demand for paper

Design by Ronald Grierson for Campbell Fabrics, about 1934.

signed by Ilonka Karasz for Donald Deskey and another in a dining room by Gilbert Rohde. By 1936 papers decorated with designs of flowers, shells and other motifs were in demand and one amateur decorator filled with misguided enthusiasm papered a room with a design in all its colour variations in alternating strips. With a larger production and better designers, the American manufacturers were in a position to export patterned papers to Europe, Kelso being the London agent for Katzenbach and Warren and Richard Thibaut, Inc. It was not long however before the English manufacturers found it profitable to revive some mid nineteenth-century designs in view of the revival of Victoriana—one charming design of a large bouquet of mixed flowers, including cabbage roses, printed in clear tones, became particularly popular.

TEXTILES

The majority of the "Modernistic" interiors featured in the periodicals of the first five years of the thirties had a sameness about them and a lack of character which made it difficult to distinguish the work of one designer from that of another. The use of the same woods, the preponderance of built-in furniture, the use of strict geometric shapes, the lack of any ornament in the way of carving or even mouldings and the use of plain or only slightly patterned fabrics for curtains and upholstery—all these factors tended to give the anonymous look of hotel rooms to most interiors. Very often the only decorative object was a rug or carpet, which almost invariably turned out to have been designed by Marion Dorn. Unfortunately it is not likely that many of her rugs have survived as, in the nature of things, the floor coverings receive the most wear of the furnishing of a room, and also in the years of reaction against Modernism her designs are most likely to have been rejected by interior decorators in favour of Aubusson or other period rugs. To judge from photographs her output must have been considerable and the standard of design extremely high. The prime requisite for a Dorn carpet—and the same applied to those designed by her husband E. McKnight Kauffer—was that the design should lie flat

between these extremes that many firms destroyed the woodblocks dating from the mid nineteenth century onwards, as it was considered that there was so little chance of their ever coming back into fashion that there was no point in continuing to store them. One firm used the blocks cut from designs ranging from Pugin to Marie Laurencin to construct a new wooden floor in the workrooms.

Sooner or later there was bound to be a reaction against the plain walls fashionable in the early thirties with a return to the use of patterned wallpapers. A contemporary reference attributes the revival of patterned papers—that is, the use of commissioned new designs—to American sources about 1934 or 1935. Corroboration for this can be found in the *Studio Year Book of Decorative Art* for 1935 where the only rooms featuring patterned papers are American—one de-

Hand-tufted carpet designed by Marion Dorn, made by Wilton Royal Wessex in the early 1930s.

on the floor and that there should be no appearance of "hills or valleys". Three-dimensional effects were eschewed and the colours were kept in a subdued tonal range. Each season she produced a new range of designs and when a design had been repeated several times it was discarded—in this way each carpet became one of a severely limited edition. The colour range may have been restricted but within those restrictions the shades were extremely subtle and were chosen with great care from a range of five hundred specially dyed. Six shades of white and three of black were used in combination with dozens of browns, beiges and greys while blues, dull orange and red were sparingly employed for accents in a decorative motif. One design, woven in carpets up to thirty feet (nine metres) square, was of a large all-over pattern reminiscent of Chinese Chippendale and executed in a technique of cut and uncut pile. Syrie Maugham used this pattern in a number of interiors in either off-white or dark brown.

The work of Allan Walton and the Edinburgh Weavers in presenting the designs of artists as applied to printed and woven fabrics received considerable publicity in decorating magazines and articles. They printed, for example, a number of designs by Duncan Grant on linen and velveteen. But the output from Walton's workshops or from the studios of the suc-

cessful textile designer Phyllis Barron was negligible compared to that of the big commercial mills where the sale of less than 10,000 yards of printed material meant that that design was a failure; a successful pattern was reckoned as selling more than 60,000 yards. For financial reasons modern designs were to be found mainly in woven fabrics—in 1936 it was calculated that 90 per cent of woven fabrics were of modern design—as the cost of the cards necessary for a new pattern on a Jacquard loom was a fraction of that of machine blocks for a printed fabric. There was a steady demand not only in England but also from America and Germany

Above: "The Little Urn", screen-printed spun satin designed by Duncan Grant in about 1933 and made by Allan Walton Textiles, London.

Right: Part of the music room designed by Duncan Grant and Vanessa Bell which was shown at the Alex Reid and Lefevre Gallery, London, 1933.

for the traditional floral patterns of the eighteenth or nineteenth centuries or for variations on these originals.

In France tapestry weaving had a hard struggle to maintain its existence in the thirties. For decades

previously the reputations of the Aubusson, Beauvais and Gobelins works had been declining. This state of affairs was due to the policy of the directors of these workshops: that of commissioning cartoons from the older generation of established painters, often from those with little or no experience of the techniques of tapestry weaving, painters who conceived a tapestry in terms of a woven version of a painting to be reproduced with absolute fidelity to the smallest nuances of colour and even brushwork. This tradition had been followed since the eighteenth century—the tapestries designed by Mignard, Coypel, Oudry or Boucher may be cited as examples—but by the early years of the twentieth century the standard of works commissioned or adapted had fallen to an extremely low level. Jean Lurçat records that in 1918 Gustave Geffroy, the director of the Gobelins factory, showed him with considerable pride a newly completed tapestry, "The Sleeping Beauty", by Jean Weber, the caricaturist of the comic journal *Le Rire* (though in fairness it must be added that at the same time Lurçat was also shown a tapestry from a painting by Odilon Redon).

This ignorance of technique on the part of designers had a direct effect on the financial state of the workshops. The technical dexterity in reproducing paintings led to the increase in the number of shades of colour required for each tapestry. The fourteenth-century masterpiece "The Apocalypse of Angers" used an extremely small number of colours—seventeen according to some authorities, twenty-two according to others. By 1740 the number used on tapestries had risen to 333, fifty years later to 587 and in 1900 some nine hundred colours were available. In the early twenties a tapestry from a design by Paul Véra required 2,667 shades and still later, through the experiments of the chemist Chevill, the Gobelins and Beauvais works were able to put at the disposition of their designers no less than 14,400 shades. The majority of these were of course of chemical origin and were found to be fugitive, so that with the passage of time many of the tapestries became travesties of the original design, large areas of the paler colours fading into a monotone. The most serious aspect of this proliferation of colours was that the cost of a tapestry became almost prohibitive, the minimum quantity of wool or silk to be dyed in a particular shade being often far more than was required.

The Gobelins and Beauvais works, under the direction of Gustave Geffroy and later of Guillaume Janneau, were subsidized by the government, but the Aubusson factory, an assemblage of private looms each working for its own clientele, was not so fortunate, and with the need to consider costs the weaving tended to be coarser than that of its rivals. The town of Aubusson with a small population of four to five thousand, a town difficult of access and dependent on its tapestry workshops, was severely hit by the crisis of 1929 and the imposition of high customs tariffs by America and other countries to which it exported a large part of its production.

But in 1929 an attempt to correct the decline of the Aubusson workshops was made by Mme Cuttoli. The wife of a French senator and a friend and patron of many of the younger generation of painters, some of whom were still struggling for recognition, she courageously invited a number of them to submit designs to be woven as tapestries. Among the first were Rouault's "Three Clowns" and works by Coutaud, Marcoussis and Lurçat. The last who, more than any of the artists invited, became involved in the designing of tapestry, records that only he and Coutaud submitted cartoons that respected the limitations and techniques of the craft and implies that his colleagues merely submitted easel paintings which were reproduced with exact fidelity with the addition of a border simulating a frame. Between 1933 and 1936 tapestries by Matisse ("Papéete"), Léger, Derain, Dufy, Braque, Segonzac, Miró and Picasso ("Two Seated Women") were added to the collection of the Atelier Cuttoli which was exhibited in Brussels, London, Stockholm and in 1936 in New York (at the Bignou Galleries), Chicago and San Francisco.

The tours were a critical success. Many who had found it difficult to enjoy abstract painting could see a meaning, for decorative purposes, in the bright colours of these tapestries. "The less definite outlines of woven threads made harmony out of discord for these few benighted ones who had not yet captured the full glory of the modern French painters' canvases," wrote an American critic and it is recorded that the Braque

Mme Cuttoli's drawing room, 1937: the mirrored fireplace is flanked by tapestries by Jean Lurçat.

found a purchaser in Chicago and the Picasso and the Rouault in Philadelphia. Mme Cuttoli's own apartment in Paris—"a modern Hôtel Sévigné"—was used as a setting for the tapestries. Two floor-to-ceiling panels by Lurçat flanked a simple mantelpiece covered in mirror. Two modern chairs covered in a beige tapestry also by Lurçat, a Louis XV table, a Chinese lacquer table and modern tables of glass, gilded copper and black lacquer were to be found in the salon, whose walls of natural oak veneer were enhanced by smaller tapestries by Picasso, Braque and Rouault. In the dining room a large Hispano Moresque chest, a Louis XIII dining table and chairs were combined with a Dufy panel.

Several factors may have contributed to the new spirit which began to find expression in the Aubusson workshops and in the Gobelins and Beauvais works —the Manufactures Nationales—in 1936. By then the general feeling was that the years of depression were over, restrictions were easing and doubtless the success of the Cuttoli venture was a cause for optimism. Reforms were inaugurated in both state and private workshops. There was a backlog of orders and assigned cartoons to be completed before the reforms could be fully realized, but by 1938 a special laboratory was licensed to prepare vegetable dyes which, like those used in the fourteenth and fifteenth centuries, would hold their colour: plantations of madder-wort at Carpentras, yellow-weed in Normandy and woad in Albi were inaugurated and the number of shades to be used in the future was drastically reduced. François

i. da Silva Bruhns – 1930

da Silva Bruhns

120

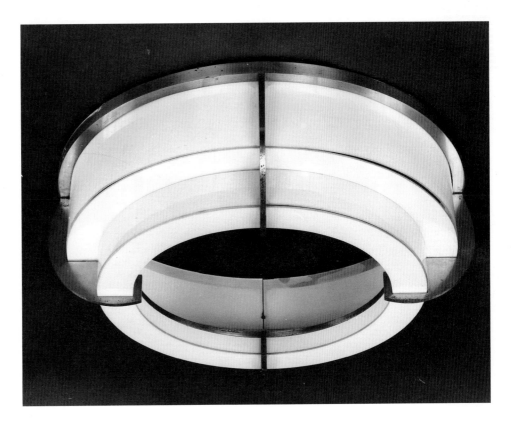

Tabard working with Jean Lurçat energetically started the reorganization of work at Aubusson just as the war started. A prisoner from 1940 to 1945, he was not able fully to realize his plans until the late 1940s when the great series of tapestries after designs by Lurçat, Dufy, Gromaire, Coutaud and others brought a new lustre to the Aubusson workshops.

LIGHTING

The comments in several volumes written in the mid thirties provide a striking reminder that electricity as a source of illumination was by no means common in England and, in those districts where it was available, it was expensive. In 1934 A. B. Read made the optimistic prophecy that "to keep within the most convenient bounds of probability, the design of artificial illumination should be examined in terms of electricity. We are now at the beginning of a new age of power, the age of clean and abundant power for the Grid is completed

and it is only a question of time before archaic methods of generating power and providing artificial light disappear. This will mean that our towns and cities and countryside will escape for ever from smuts and soot and fumes; that by day we shall get more and clearer sunlight, and by night more abundant light. Electricity will be available in most parts of the country at a reasonable cost in time." But "this cannot happen at once, unfortunately." And indeed, "it is not everyone who can afford, or who likes this form of illumination," wrote Mrs Darcy Braddell a year later.

A storm of protest had met the erection throughout the countryside of the pylons carrying the high-voltage transmission lines of the Grid, which was designed to reduce the cost of electricity and to bring new power to districts which had hitherto been dependent upon gas, candles or oil lamps as sources of illumination. The high cost of electricity imposed the need for utilizing it to the utmost once it had been installed, and bulbs were often left unshaded so that the light was not wasted. The tendency was, however,

Above left: Hand-tufted carpet designed by Edward McKnight Kauffer, made by Wilton Royal Wessex in about 1930.

Left: Design for a carpet for the Maharajah of Indore by Da Silva Bruhns, 1930.

Right: Metal and glass ceiling light by Jean Perzel, about 1935.

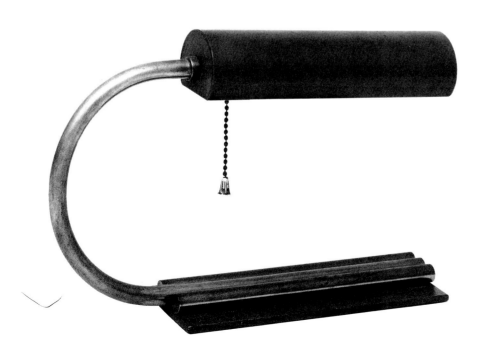

Above left: Chromium-plated metal and glass table lamp by Desny, early 1930s.

Above: Aluminium desk lamp by Jacques Le Chevalier, early 1930s.

Left: Desk lamp by Gilbert Rohde of patinated metal, made in about 1933 by the Mutual Sunset Lamp Manufacturing Co. of Brooklyn, New York.

to disguise electric fittings wherever possible and purists in design fulminated against the "nice little electric 'candle' dripping with immovable wax", or "the worst shapes of the earliest gas chandeliers incorporated in the design of electric lights". In a majority of cases the concept of the traditional centre light was prevalent, even if the design of the fitting was in the latest idiom of chrome and pearl glass, and in the average home the advantages of more convenient and incidentally more flattering table or standard lamps were not fully realized. Catalogues of the latest designs in fittings for domestic use throughout the thirties show a preponderance of centre lights and wall brackets, usually in fan shapes of tinted glass, standard lamps being in the minority. The need for economy is reflected in the advice that "it should be remembered that walls and ceilings must be coloured to help the lighting of rooms, if we wish to be intelligently economical. Clean pale colours reflect most light and it is expensive to supplement light in rooms whose surfaces are dull and dark in tone, while indirect lighting with the source of light altogether hidden practically doubles the consumption of current, and unless properly used it has rather a drowsy appearance."

The arid appearance of many interiors of the early thirties and especially those put forward as examples of the new school of fitness for purpose is due in part to the institutional character of many of the "functional" electric light fittings with their globes of opaque glass held in sockets of chromium- or nickel-plated steel. Designed to be practical, easy to maintain and clean, they succeeded in giving a dispiriting light to an interior and with the advent of period revivalism they were relegated to serve a purely functional purpose in public buildings or institutions where the designs originating in the thirties can still be found.

For those to whom economy was not a pressing consideration or for those looking for more decorative light fittings, the recourse seems to have been to import them from the Continent, from Italy, France or Czechoslovakia. To judge from the large number still current, light fittings of moulded glass by Lalique or Sabino appear to have been sold in England in considerable quantities.

Lampshades of pleated parchment held together by silk cords, or shades of vellum or parchment sewn on to a metal frame with leather thongs, had made their appearance in the twenties and became even more popular in the following decade, sometimes being painted with "jazz" motifs. For the more conservative period interiors a decorative silk shade on a Chinese pottery or celadon vase or on a figure of semi-precious stone was still considered essential.

GLASS

The large plate-glass windows, often stretching from floor to ceiling, which characterized many of the buildings designed on the Continent or in America by Mies van der Rohe, Hans Schumacher, Le Corbusier and their followers, were not popular in England. The implied lack of privacy and the climate of a country where it was considered preferable to be out in the landscape rather than to sit and look at it inhibited English architects from incorporating glass walls into the comparatively few examples of modern architecture erected during the thirties in England. Even in public buildings the tendency was to design windows broken up into smaller panes. Equally, the glass bricks used by many American architects do not seem to have attracted the same attention in England or France, and the possibilities of their being used as internal partitions or in place of clear glass windows to mask an ugly outlook were ignored. Their structural strength and decorative qualities were more than outweighed, in the view of most British architects and builders, by the fact that they were not a traditional material and by their greater cost.

Inside the house it was a different matter and architects and interior decorators made full use of the new varieties of glass manufactured during the thirties. There were many historical precedents for rooms with the walls and ceilings covered in mirrors, but limitations of size of the pieces of glass had required the provision of some sort of decorative framework to conceal the joins. With improved techniques of manufacture sheets of mirror-glass could be made sufficiently large to give an uninterrupted reflection. In this way a comparatively small room could be made

to appear twice as large by the aid of one wall covered with mirror—a desirable effect when, for economic reasons, people were tending to live in smaller apartments. Large areas of mirror were particularly useful in the small rooms which were a feature of the new blocks of apartments built in the thirties. The size of the new one-room flats—a euphemism for a bed-sitting room with attached bathroom—could be made to appear greater by judiciously placed sheets of mirror and at the same time the light which filtered through the net curtains, necessary in towns for reasons of privacy, could be reflected.

The dining tables made by Lalique and Sabino utilized glass in a different way, less to exploit the transparency of the material than for the sake of its decorative possibilities. The practical difficulties of invisibly joining a transparent table top to an equally transparent base were avoided by the use of an inconspicuous metal framework, finished in chromium plate, which supported a number of repeated glass units ornamented by sand-blasting, the single sheet of

glass forming the table top being similarly treated on the underside.

Reeded and fluted glass, plain or silvered, was used a great deal in bathrooms. Probably the most publicized use of this type of glass was in the bathroom designed for Mrs Edward James (Miss Tilly Losch) by Paul Nash, where the walls were faced with panels of metallic purple, pale rose and black glass of different textures arranged in abstract designs. Bathrooms in the twenties had usually been purely functional, despite the exotic examples designed for movies featuring Gloria Swanson, Pola Negri and other vamps. Tiled walls and a wooden casing around the bath were often the sole concessions to decoration, while exposed plumbing and a gas heater were common. But in the thirties a greater use of central heating, and technical improvements both in the function and appearance of plumbing units, encouraged the possibilities of decorating the bathroom as carefully as the rest of the house, and a number of bathrooms such as Mrs James's, decorated wholly or partly in mirrors,

Left: Glass chandelier made in Murano, Venice, in the mid 1930s, and sold by Veronese from their shop in the rue St Philippe-du-Roule, Paris. It has a metal frame, with the light fitting concealed in a silvered bowl, from which the curved glass strips cascade out in the shape of a fountain.

Right: Glass-lined bathroom designed by Paul Nash in 1932 and made by James Clark, Eaton & Son. It was commissioned by the collector Edward James for his wife, Tilly Losch.

received considerable publicity. Coloured mirrors—gold, gunmetal, green, blue, red—were extensively used in bathrooms, as well as in restaurants, but by far the most popular colour was peach with its flattering reflections.

Sigmund Pollitzer in England and Max Ingrand in Paris were among the designers of engraved mirrors or glass used for decoration in restaurants and private apartments, the former working in a calligraphic manner, the latter experimenting more widely in coloured textures of gold and black to enhance the engraved designs. Max Ingrand's work was widely used in France, America and England. In America Joseph Urban, the Frankl Galleries, Donald Deskey and Gilbert Rohde all made use of a large frameless circular mirror, three to four feet (about one metre) in diameter and applied directly to the wall, to lend to a room the dramatic note which was already becoming a characteristic of American interior decoration.

Pilkington Brothers' stand at the Dorland House Exhibition, designed by Oliver Hill, demonstrated the

Above: Elevator foyer designed by Kerstin Taube for a New York apartment and made by Robert Pichenot in the early 1930s; the Manhattan skyline is painted on mirror-glass in monochrome tones shading from silver to black. A false ceiling of frosted glass, banded with aluminium and concealing the lights, was designed by Walter Kantack.

Left: New York dining room decorated by Inez Croom of Nancy McClelland Inc in the early 1930s. The cornice, fireplace surround, panel above the door and the table top are all of mirror-glass. Dining rooms diminished in size during the 1930s, occasionally dwindling to nothing more than an alcove off the living room, and dining tables rarely seated more than six.

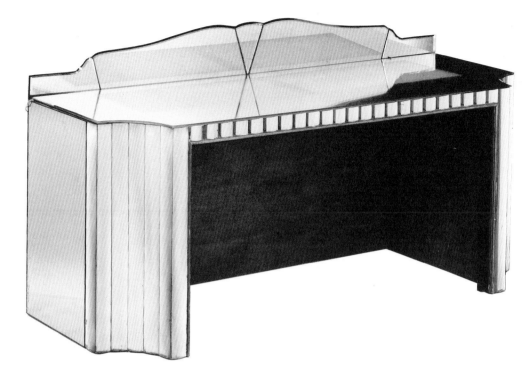

Left: Side table faced in mirror-glass, designer unknown, about 1935.

Below: Exhibit designed by Oliver Hill for Pilkington Brothers made entirely of glass and shown in the Dorland Hall Exhibition of 1933.

many possibilities afforded by new types of glass, from the floor with its tiles of glass and mosaic patterns of gold and mirror to the walls of panels of ribbed and obscured mirror, with sand-blasted or engraved decorations. The furniture—a chaise-longue, a dressing table and stool and a small table—was entirely made from curved and shaped sheets of plate glass. These were made primarily as showpieces for the exhibition and their practical application was limited—not many people would have had the courage to relax on the glass chaise-longue supported by four glass balls—but they were the forerunners of similar furniture realized in lighter plastics.

Another form of glass extant in the thirties was Vitrolite, an opaque glass with a smooth face and a back ridged to facilitate fixing with a mastic compound. Vitrolite was made in a number of colours as well as black and white but the insipidity of most of the shades and its rather uninteresting texture limited its general use to restaurants and other places where an easily cleaned surface was desirable. The black Vitrolite, however, was very widely used as a contrast in conjunction with white or peach mirror.

The wide and varied use of mirror to cover pieces

Right: Cocktail bar designed by Kenneth Cheesman and made by the British Vitrolite Co., London, in the early 1930s to show the decorative possibilities of their opaque glass. The circular plaque of rough-cast glass was designed by Sigmund Pollitzer.

Below: Dressing table by Robert Block, made by the Société Industrielle d'Art, Paris, in about 1935.

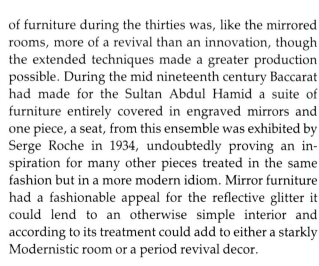

of furniture during the thirties was, like the mirrored rooms, more of a revival than an innovation, though the extended techniques made a greater production possible. During the mid nineteenth century Baccarat had made for the Sultan Abdul Hamid a suite of furniture entirely covered in engraved mirrors and one piece, a seat, from this ensemble was exhibited by Serge Roche in 1934, undoubtedly proving an inspiration for many other pieces treated in the same fashion but in a more modern idiom. Mirror furniture had a fashionable appeal for the reflective glitter it could lend to an otherwise simple interior and according to its treatment could add to either a starkly Modernistic room or a period revival decor.

Robert Block, director of the Studio Athelia at Aux Trois Quartiers, designed Modernist furniture in mirror-glass, manufactured by La Société Industrielle d'Art. Typical designs were plain, angular and undecorated, in clear or tinted mirror-glass. He also designed such pieces as a commode in which Modernism gave way to period references—the carcass, stripped of its covering of antiqued mirror engraved on the back with gilt lines and arabesques, could be that of a French or Italian commode of the late eighteenth century. Commodes of this type, together with low tables, bedside tables and cigarette boxes covered in mirror, were sold by Fortnum and Mason from 1935 until 1939.

Furniture covered in peach-coloured mirror was extremely popular in England in the mid thirties, especially the cocktail cabinets which were a necessary furnishing in upper middle-class homes. The problem of covering a curved surface with mirror was solved by the use of Vitroflex, a strong, closely woven fabric upon which were glued small squares or rectangles of thin mirror. The flexibility of the supporting fabric enabled Vitroflex to be glued to convex surfaces or even to columns of comparatively small diameter, the small facets of mirror giving a brilliantly glittering effect.

Leslie and Edgar Mendenhall designed for James Clark, Eaton & Son a number of pieces of mirror furniture using shaped and engraved mirrors, which, to quote from a current advertisement, "truly reflected the spirit of the new fashion, sophisticatedly modern it is very individual and distinctive." Cigarette boxes covered in white mirror with a chrome-plated bar handle were on sale at the London firm of Droods in 1935 for 7s 6d.

Serge Roche, a connoisseur with a fastidious appreciation of quality allied to an appreciation of the more fantastic aspects of seventeenth- and eighteenth-century art, in 1934 exhibited a collection of purely decorative objects. Made to his own design, they were deliberately calculated to serve no practical function but simply "to animate space". Although the exhibition contained a number of pieces of furniture which could be considered functional—commodes, consoles, light fixtures—their treatment was such that they were intended to be regarded as decorative objects to provoke admiration or to stimulate the imagination. Mantelpieces, stools, centrepieces for dining tables with period references to French or Italian baroque, were covered with faceted mirrors, as were large and small obelisks—a decorative accessory much in favour during the thirties. The mirror used to ornament these objects was often given an artificial antique effect similar to that caused by age on the mercury-backed mirrors made before the mid nineteenth century when silver replaced mercury. One mirror, half sunburst, half sunflower, was designed by Serge Roche in 1936 and showed an ingenious use of small pieces of mirror to cover a curved surface.

René Lalique was one designer who was unaffected by the enforced austerity. He alone of the French glassmakers maintained his position during the Depression period and was even able to increase his repertoire of stock designs. This was probably due to the fact that as most of his products in addition to being beautiful were also practical, they were ideally suited for wedding presents or presentation gifts. Among the gifts made to George VI and Queen Elizabeth on the occasion of their state visit to Paris was a set of table glass, candelabras and a screen by Lalique, ornamented with motifs of birds. A glass fountain by Lalique was featured in the Main Hall of Olympia during the 1931 Daily Mail Ideal Home Exhibition and in the same year a glass chapel was one of the exhibits at the Salon d'Automne in Paris. In June 1933 Lalique was honoured by a retrospective exhibition at the Pavillon de Marsan which embraced the entire scope of his work from the beautiful and fantastic jewelry in the Art Nouveau style dating from around 1900 to his latest designs for glass.

An extensive catalogue of Lalique's work published in 1932 and a number of illustrated advertisements by the Breves Gallery (Lalique's representatives in London) are of some assistance in helping to ascribe dates to the different designs, although the problem is complicated in that a number of models appear to have been in continuous production. As Lalique glass is not dated, the only way to gauge the sequence of design is by comparison of references in periodicals or advertisements and by elimination to establish the earliest date—a method which still leaves room for speculation. An article in *The Studio* for 1931 established the fact that the majority of his motor car mascots were designed before that date, though a further complication is added in that the "Hawk" mascot was also adapted as a decorative handle to a vase in dark brown glass. From documentary evidence a date no later than 1934 can be applied to the design of the small dining table of engraved glass on a chromium-plated metal framework which is in the collection of the Brighton Museum. Lalique glass, although never inexpensive, was produced in such quantities as almost to warrant the description of being mass-produced. Large prestige pieces such as this table, however, were made in limited quantities. A similar table made by Sabino was illustrated in an advertisement in *The Studio Year Book of Decorative Art* for 1931.

Maurice Marinot consolidated a reputation

Black and white glass vases designed by Frederick Carver for the Stueben division of the old Corning Glass Works, New York State, and first produced in about 1925.

Above: Engraved glass vase by Keith Murray for Stevens and Williams, late 1930s. Murray designed several pieces for the firm, both decorative and utilitarian.

Right: Glass bottle and stopper by Maurice Marinot, deep etched with angular motifs, 1931; formerly in the collection of the celebrated bronze founder Adrien Hebrand.

established in the twenties as an unrivalled mastercraftsman in glass. He developed a number of techniques, including that of imprisoning between two layers of glass another layer evenly interspersed with bubbles, or layers of speckled colour. In 1937 he abandoned his work in this field after a career lasting a quarter of a century and returned to his first love, painting.

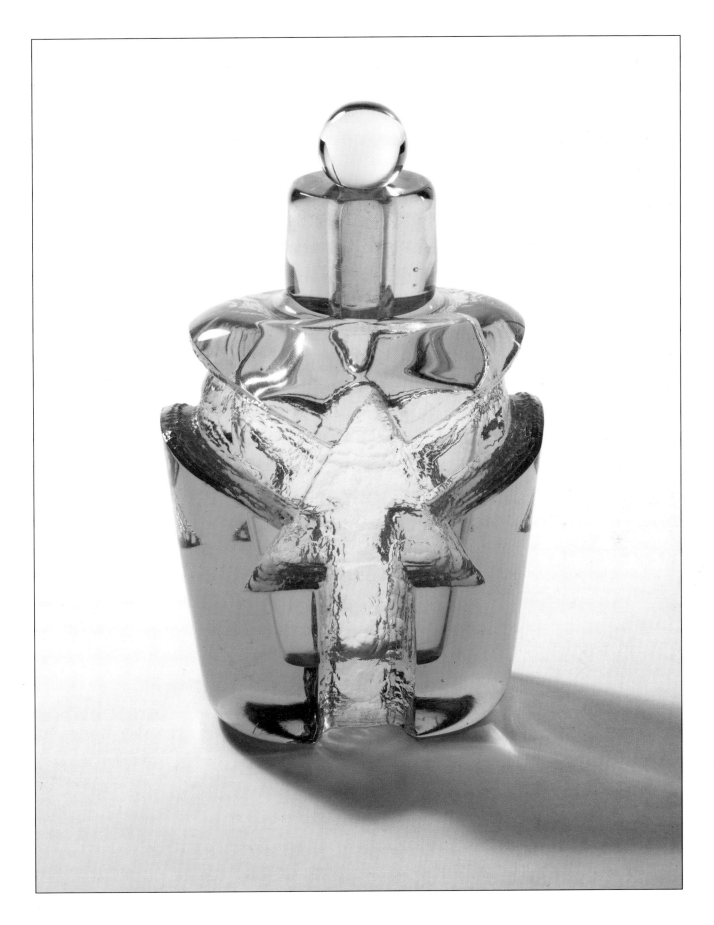

In England, W. Clyne Farquharson, designing for Walsh and Walsh, and Keith Murray for Stevens and Williams, created simple vessels in colourless glass, engraved with elegant, restrained, decorative designs. Their efforts were isolated instances in contrast with the ever-popular variety which earned the scorn of the purists by an over-abundance of faceting applied to poorly designed forms. "Design still dies the death of a thousand cuts . . . the cocktail has a lot to answer for: much spurious modernism has been inspired by it and most of us have shuddered as we have imbibed from glasses designed in a spirit of squalid gaiety," wrote John Gloag in *Industrial Art Explained*, deploring the fact that examples of restrained design such as Keith Murray's were "isolated instances".

In America, the glass produced by the Steuben glass division of the old Corning Glass Works in 1932 was greeted with lyrical enthusiasm by Augusta Owen Patterson in *Town and Country*. She found "in these undecorated shapes a certain likeness to the tall blossoms of the yucca when the moonlight illumines its particle of bloom, giving a translucency to the whiteness which appeals to the emotions and stimulates the imagination", and further described it as "having the quality of moonlight congratulating a white flower on its perishable attractions". On a more mundane level, these hand-made vases, bowls and candle-holders, some with the opaque white glass outlined with a thread of black glass, were of simple shapes, sometimes reminiscent of those found in Chinese glass, while the urns, finished with black handles, were "of that flexible, all-enduring type which is entirely *en règle* with the Directoire, English Regency and our new fabricated Victorian . . . or it can take its place with the more rebellious Twentieth Century inventions."

Blown-glass figures were considered especially suitable ornaments for Modernist interiors during the early part of the decade. These could include ballet dancers, acrobats, black musicians and whimsical animals by Marianne von Allesch of New York, J. Brychta in Czechoslovakia, Guido Balsamo Stella and Venini and Company in Italy, and Fritz Lampl of Vienna.

CERAMICS

The Studio Year Book for 1931 comments that "on the Continent dinner services are getting simpler and simpler" and the porcelain designed by Suzanne Lalique (René's daughter), Jean Luce and Marcel Goupy reflects this trend to leave the surface unadorned but for a discreet geometrical ornament or banding in silver combined with a monogram. While the work of these three designers cannot be considered as produced for the popular market, the difference between "popular" taste in England and Germany is exemplified by the experiment conducted by the Berlin State Porcelain factory in 1930. One hundred and fifty cups of all periods were gathered from museums and collections and visitors to the exhibition were asked to vote as to their preferences for design and ornament as guidance for the development of future designs. By a large majority the favourite was a simple white cup modelled by Wegely for the Berlin factory about 1750, with a classic white cup of the Empire period, equally simple, as second choice. It is safe to say that a similar opinion poll conducted in England would have had a very different result, the taste of the general public, as reflected in trade advertisements, veering more to elaborate shapes over-decorated with ineptly drawn floral motifs.

In the early thirties the jazzing-up process deplored by Paul Nash brought about some eccentric conceptions in the field of commercial ceramics in England. The most fragile of household equipment, pottery and porcelain, absorbed a considerable number of new designs each year, as the manufacturers tempted the public to buy a complete tea or dinner service in an enticing new design rather than replace the broken items of a service in use for some time and consequently over-familiar. Attempting to fit in with the Modernistic feeling, manufacturers in France and England experimented with a variety of geometrical shapes which, if not as handsome or as practical as the traditional ones, were at least different and indicated to the public that the industry was keeping up with the times.

For economic reasons, the curved shapes inherited or derived from eighteenth-century models still formed the greater part of the production of most potteries but these were decorated with geometrical designs which generally failed to harmonize with the shapes to which they were applied. "New concepts in tableware", however, appeared in the shape of square, spoutless teapots with recessed handles—an original idea but incurring the disadvantages of scalded knuckles and erratic flow of tea; square cups and saucers—an experiment which died an early death; combined saucer and plate with a depression to take a cup, another concept which failed to attract, and eccentrically designed handles to cups, some solid, some triangular, but all guaranteed to make holding a cup filled with liquid a hazardous venture. One of the more successful of these designs was the "Vogue" pattern tea sets by the Shelley Potteries of which a writer in the *Pottery Gazette and Glass Trade Review* for March 1931 commented, "their record for the last few years has provided the dealer with abundant evidence that there is no standing still at the Shelley Potteries", an opinion echoed by the statement in *Woman and Beauty* in the same year that "the china that is making

Ceramic sculpture by S. Nicholson Babb, 1932.

the tea tray in a smart house as much a matter of fashion as the hostess's gown can be seen in the 1931 shapes and new designs of utter modernity". In the majority of cases the determined, even frantic, efforts to conform to "utter modernity" failed to fulfil the hopes of their creators and the public response was cool, preference still being shown for floral designs and conservative shapes. The greater proportion of commercial pottery and porcelain, apart from replicas of traditional patterns, was of a low standard of design ranging from the blatantly ugly to the anaemically refined, and designs similar to those of Suzanne Lalique, Jean Luce and Marcel Goupy in France and Susie Cooper and Keith Murray in England were the exception rather than the rule. The city of Stoke-on-Trent's school of art had departments at Burslem, Hanley, Stoke and Langton, all under the experienced guidance of Gordon Forsyth and all these departments worked in close connection with the pottery manufacturers in the district. The students, after five years' tuition, were all absorbed into the industry, an excep-

tional state of affairs in the economic conditions of the early thirties, but almost without exception they were employed as executants and not as designers. As Josiah Wedgwood pointed out in *Industrial Design* in 1934, "Movements in pottery design generally start on the Continent, spreading to London five years afterwards, to the provinces three years after that and to the USA still later"—a surprising statement but one which, coming from such an authoritative source, can hardly be doubted. The Wedgwood company entrusted the design of their contemporary production to Keith Murray whose simple and elegant vases, if sometimes rather unmemorable, received considerable publicity and, from the praise accorded them by

Below: Earthenware vases designed by Keith Murray for Josiah Wedgwood & Sons of Etruria. Murray's designs for Wedgwood were hand-thrown and in some cases revived the use of engine-turning, but were inexpensive, even for the time. They were coloured in subdued tones of green, white, grey and buff.

Right: Decorative charger designed by Clarice Cliff and made by the Newport Pottery, about 1935.

various writers, seemed to fulfil all the current standards of fitness for purpose. In France, incidentally, Jean Luce was producing a range of vases which bore a close resemblance to those of Keith Murray.

"A few well-chosen pieces of Miss Clarice Cliff's 'Bizarre' ware seem just to add the last touch of distinction to a carefully thought out room," ran the text of a 1934 advertisement in the *Illustrated London News*. Clarice Cliff, born in 1900, was trained in all branches of pottery-making, including modelling, at Burslem School of Art before she joined the Burslem firm of A. J. Wilkinson as an apprentice, together with her two sisters. She was given every encouragement to develop her very original ideas and when she retired in 1939 she was Art Director of Wilkinsons and the subsidiary firm of the Newport Pottery Company. In addition to the "Bizarre" ware, she originated "Scarab Blue Inspiration Bizarre" ware, "Delecia",

Earthenware jug by Bernard Leach, St Ives, about 1930.

"Patina" and a number of patterns like "Crocus" and "My Garden", which were executed in on-glaze technique by Clarice Cliff personally or by the assistants she trained. The designs ranged from the fairly conventional "Crocus" pattern to vases, bowls and large decorative plates boldly ornamented with abstract geometrical designs or arrangements of conventionalized flowers in vivid colourings of orange, blue, yellow and black. "Bizarre" ware achieved extreme popularity and the pieces were in great favour as wedding presents.

The thirties was not an encouraging period for the studio potters. Too great a dependence on Chinese, Korean or Japanese models as sources of inspiration tended to develop a certain sameness and family resemblance between the products of different potters and the limited clientele for this type of craft diminished during the Depression. The expenditure of time and the outlay on materials beyond the original cost of equipment for throwing and firing the pots was barely compensated by the low prices to be obtained for the finished products, and a further deterrent was that the conventional classic shapes and coloured glazes bore close resemblances to original oriental pieces which could be found in considerable numbers at the same or even lower prices. Although it was asserted that studio pottery eventually influenced commercial pottery—a statement which could be accepted with reservations—the commercial designers were on the whole more adventurous in their designs, especially where the basic shape of the vessel was concerned.

The doyen of British potters, Bernard Leach, is recorded as having suffered considerable hardship during the thirties and in 1934 he closed his small pottery in South Devon and together with his Japanese assistant Shoji Hamada returned to Japan, where his reputation was high among connoisseurs and collectors. He returned to England in 1936. Leach's former pupil, Michael Cardew, worked at the Winchcombe pottery which he had founded in 1926 and William Staite-Murray continued his work, but there are few instances of new talent appearing on the scene. The small demand for studio pottery was more than adequately supplied by the established crafts-

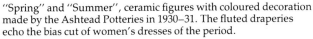

"Spring" and "Summer", ceramic figures with coloured decoration made by the Ashstead Potteries in 1930–31. The fluted draperies echo the bias cut of women's dresses of the period.

PLASTICS

The early thirties saw the production of plastic ware on a commercial scale. Non-inflammable and unaffected by hot water, the tableware produced by Beatl Sales Ltd about 1930 had the added advantage of being almost unbreakable, was without smell and did not alter the taste of the food or drink it contained. Marketed under the name "Linga-Longa" ware, it was manufactured from a non-phenolic synthetic resin and could be finished in a variety of marbled and

men. The Ashstead Potteries, founded after the First World War to give employment to disabled ex-servicemen, extended their range of white glazed ware to include decorative figures of which "Spring" and "Summer", modelled by Joan Pyman in 1930 and 1931 respectively, are good examples.

137

mottled effects. Its low cost of production ensured a ready sale in the cheaper markets—it was particularly in demand for picnic baskets—but its rather unattractive colourings and the "feel" of the material limited its appeal and ensured that it did not become a serious rival to the pottery or porcelain trades. Experiments in the Imperial Chemical Industries Ltd Laboratories resulted in a transparent plastic, white or coloured, which could be moulded under heat into different forms: complete articles could be shaped in steel moulds, flat boards could be pressed and laminated to other materials, and plastics could be produced in blocks which could subsequently be shaped by trimming or cutting. Such a material obviously offered new possibilities but nobody seems to have known quite what to do with it, though a certain amount of clear plastic furniture of small dimensions—chairs, coffee tables and so on—was made in the United States, more for exhibition purposes than for practical use. The presses and moulds used for its production were extremely expensive and consequently the material needed to be sold in extremely large quantities to cover the initial costs. Though it was ideal for con-

tainers for beauty products, for instance, the cosmetic industry was reluctant to experiment in bulk in case this new and untried material should develop idiosyncracies after a while. It was not until a few years later, during the war, that uses were found for plastics on a large scale.

DECORATIVE SCULPTURE

It is surprising to find that coloured bronze and ivory figures had a considerable sale during the thirties. Not by any means inexpensive, they were regarded by many as jokes or suitable only for the New Rich and were entirely ignored by both the advocates of fitness for purpose and by those experimenting with period revivals. As far as can be ascertained, not a single example can be found in any of the photographs published in books or periodicals dealing with decoration during the thirties. Yet in spite of this they were sold in sufficient quantities to warrant the distributors, Phillips and MacConnal, taking a stand each year at the Ideal Home Exhibition. The catalogues of the

Left: A group of objects moulded in urea-formaldehyde in the 1930s, in forms and colours characteristic of the plastics of the period.

Right: "Con Brio", decorative sculpture by F. Preiss in cold-painted bronze and carved ivory, about 1935.

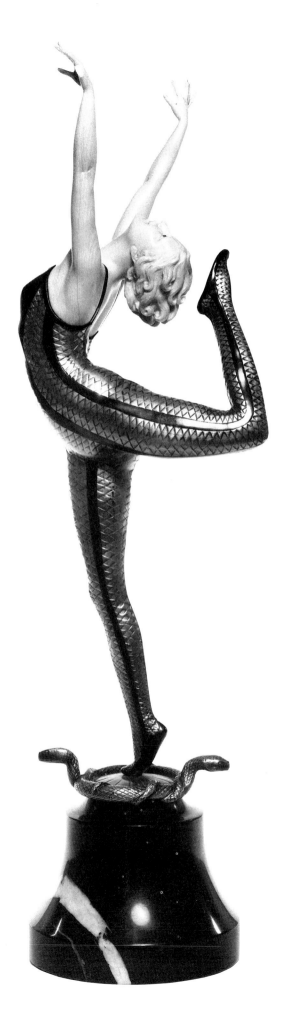

exhibition are a primary source of information as to their creators.

"Continental", generally used as a pejorative adjective, could be applied to these figures with absolute truth, for the sculptors were French, German or Austrian. Poertzel, one of the most successful, was for many years "under protection of the Duke of Coburg-Gotha" and the King of Bulgaria purchased his "Bacchanal". Another statue of Poertzel's was named "Tanz Finale". Other sculptors were F. Preiss, D. H. Chiparus, Bouraine, Paul Philippe and Pierre le Faguays, "so well known for his statues seen in the ornate palace cinemas of today".

POSTERS AND PUBLICITY

As the force of the Depression gathered strength in a series of financial crises, the need for more systematic and adroit publicity schemes on the part of manufacturers and retailers became intensified. In the face of dwindling markets the need grew for more direct and compulsive advertising and the change of title of the periodical *Posters and Publicity* to *Modern Publicity* in 1930 may be interpreted as indicative of the changing circumstances—advertising organized and adapted to meet the prevailing difficult trade circumstances. The poster became too costly as a means of drawing attention to a particular product, especially if it was printed in colours and commissioned from a well-known artist, and business concerns allocated a greater proportion of their necessarily limited budgets for advertising to space in newspapers and periodicals where it reached a wider public. The tendency was for the poster to become more of a prestige symbol than a direct means of salesmanship and "to represent a relatively small part of the business of calling attention to various goods and services", as John Gloag wrote in 1934. In spite of the enlightened policies of such

Far left: "Diana and Stag", bronze group of 1937 by David Evans, who worked in a classical tradition in contrast with the stylized decorative work of such sculptors as Preiss and Poertzel.

Left: "The Snake Charmer", decorative sculpture by Professor Poertzel in patinated bronze and carved ivory, about 1935.

organizations as Shell Petrol, the London Underground and the various branches of the railways in England, the tendency was to patronize the designers already flourishing in the twenties, Tom Purvis, Frank Newbould, Austin Cooper, Norman Wilkinson and E. McKnight Kauffer. In their different styles they had all mastered the technique of presenting a message with an immediate urgency and an economy of means comparable to the masterpieces of poster design produced by Cassandre in France. A new development influencing the design of posters was the repetition of a theme or slogan in various forms—"That's Shell, that was," "Guinness is good for you," the "Mr Therm" designed by Eric Fraser for the Gas Light and Coke Company, or the Dubonnet posters by

Poster advertising Maurice Chevalier by Charles Kiffer, 1937.

Left: Poster by Cassandre for Cook's wagon lits, 1933. This was a prestige advertisement by France's most distinguished poster designer, whose work was as well known in the 1930s as it had been in the previous decade.

Above right: Poster by McKnight Kauffer for B. P. Ethyl, 1936, incorporating photography and emphatically Modernist graphics.

Right: Edward McKnight Kauffer, photographed with his own work by George Platt-Lynes.

Cassandre which became so much a part of the Paris scene.

The situation in the United States in 1930 was a grim one for the manufacturer and national advertiser. The prevailing buyers' market was forcing prices down and the limited money available for advertising had to be disposed in such a way as to provide the best results. It is recorded that almost no manufacturers of national standing stopped advertising in 1930, but equally the standard of design was mediocre. In spite of the increasing number of commercial artists, the Art

Directors' Guild had difficulty in finding enough works out of the thousands submitted to fill the quota of 1,350 exhibits for their annual exhibition. In consequence it is understandable that French artists should have been commissioned by American firms to

Below: Poster for Shell by John Armstrong, one of a series commissioned in the early 1930s from leading British artists, including Paul Nash and Graham Sutherland.

Right: Poster advertising Green Line coaches by the French artist Jean Dupas.

EVERYWHERE YOU GO

NEWLANDS CORNER

JOHN ARMSTRONG.

YOU CAN BE SURE OF SHELL

"Thus off they went, and four-in-hand
Dash'd briskly tow'rds the promis'd land."

To-day in comfort by "Green Line" Coach

Poster advertising the Chicago World's Fair, artist unknown, 1933.

ment for Erté with whom the publication had parted company after a long association) and in 1936 he created the setting for the Balanchine version of the ballet *Aubade*—first produced in 1929 with choreography by Nijinska and settings by Jean-Michel Frank.

Modern Publicity records that the only good posters to be found in Germany were those produced in Munich and Dresden and, here again, recourse was made to French commercial artists for fashion drawings, with the added factor that as there were no

Right: One of a set of three posters by Richard Lindner for Barnes Pianos, designed in 1939 and printed in twelve colours by photolithography.

Below: Poster by Paul Colin for the Paris 1937 Exhibition.

provide style and elegance for their publicity. Saks Fifth Avenue, for instance, commissioned a series of drawings by Jean Dupas, though it is noticable that the exaggerated elongation of the female figure and the bizarre costumes characteristic of his work were modified almost to the point of conventionality. Marie Laurencin and Pierre Roy were introduced to a wider public in America through their drawings for shipping lines and wines. Mention must be made of the enterprise shown by the fashion magazines in commissioning covers drawn by de Chirico, Dali, Berman, Marie Laurencin (*Vogue* had two covers by her in one year), Pierre Roy (a number of his mysterious and magical still-lifes also appeared on *Vogue* covers during the thirties) and, of course, the omnipresent Christian Bérard. Cassandre was commissioned to design a series of twelve covers for *Harper's Bazaar* (as a replace-

Above: Advertising poster by the German artist Willrab.

Left: Advertising photograph for Osram by John Havinden, brother of the graphic artist Ashley Havinden, about 1935.

German specialists in this type of drawing the "sweet" drawings of pretty girls came from England.

As the decade advanced, the techniques of reproduction improved until the point was reached when it was no longer necessary for a poster designer to think in simplified masses of flat colour. Richard Lindner's three posters for Barnes Pianos, conceived in a neo-Victorian style in the current trend, were printed by photolithography in twelve colours in 1939 and created such a stir that Barnes were inundated by requests from the public for copies. A poster by Anna Zinkeisen for the Southern Railway, of a rather lower artistic standard, necessitated no fewer than seventeen printings—a costly process reflecting the importance attached to prestige posters at a time when the English railway system was divided into regional services, each competing to entice the holiday-going public of foreign tourists to visit the resorts and beauty spots in each region.

6

DECORATIVE PAINTERS

P ainters as much as anyone were severely affected by the Depression. The dramatic suddenness of the Wall Street Crash brought to an end a boom in Paris where Americans, with the exchange rate very much in their favour, had been lavishly buying contemporary paintings, good and bad. The periodical *L'Amour de l'Art*, with its regular feature of critical notices of the many current exhibitions, often confined its comments on the work of a painter to one derogatory word, and the paintings illustrated in these articles and in those devoted to the work of an individual painter or sculptor indicate why the reputation of the Ecole de Paris was on the decline. The remark attributed to André Lhote in 1930—"Nobody is buying paintings—painting is saved"—speaks for itself. Add to the Depression the fashion for bare walls and the prospects for artists in the early thirties were grim, and it is not surprising that many were glad to turn to commissions which in happier times they would have despised—decorative flower paintings, screens or designs for ceramics. In 1934 galleries were selling paintings by Eric Gill, C. R. W. Nevinson, Frank Dobson and Charles Ginner for £10 or less or, in one case, works by Augustus John and Sickert for £100 on instalments.

The rebuilding of many London department stores, originally an inconvenient huddle of small shops added to as neighbouring premises became available, into large and often imposing modern buildings started at the beginning of the century and con-

Left: Entrance hall designed by Allan Walton for Fortnum and Mason, London, about 1935. The walls, painted in a marbled finish in ivory and pale olive green, provide a setting for the large panel, painted on glass and intended to give an illusion of space.

Below: "Aquarius" by Jean Dupas, 1934, one of a series of oil paintings depicting the signs of the zodiac.

Preliminary study by Frank Brangwyn for the House of Lords murals, submitted to the Royal Fine Art Commission in 1930.

tinued, despite the Depression, into the thirties. Their large wall spaces began to be used for mural decorations as prestige attractions and those by Clement Cowles—a regular exhibitor at the Royal Academy —reflected the growing interest in Victoriana. It is recorded that "while the work was in progress, groups of people were always to be found watching the painting, and criticism was flattering, idiotic, or vitriolic, but always lively, which pleased the store gods by producing a 'happening' atmosphere."

FRANK BRANGWYN

The decade had opened with a major controversy in the English art world. In February 1930 a Royal Fine Arts Commission inspected five of the eighteen panels destined for the Royal Gallery in the Palace of Westminster, a scheme commissioned from the eminent painter Frank Brangwyn by Lord Iveagh and intended as a memorial to the peers who had lost their lives in the First World War. After deliberation the verdict was given that the panels were unsuitable and the scheme would not be installed. Considerable indignation was expressed in the press about this affront to the artist and to the memory of his patron—who had died three years before—but it was noticable that references to the artistic merits of the paintings were guarded and there were few comments to the effect that the members of the Commission were depriving the nation of a great masterpiece. Since 1895 when Brangwyn had painted two large panels, "Music" and "Dancing", for the entrance of Siegfried Bing's new establishment L'Art Nouveau, his reputation had always stood higher in Europe, America and Japan than in his own country (though he was born in Bruges in Belgium, his parents were both English). Particularly in the early 1900s, there were few exhibitions on the Continent which did not feature one or more of his paintings. From about the age of thirty he had led a secluded life, avoiding social intercourse and producing an enormous body of work.

The House of Lords panels were to have been both the culmination of his career and a glorification of

the riches, the natural beauties and the magnificence of the British Empire, symbolizing the heritage for which so many had died in the First World War, rather than the fact of their death. Since the work was commissioned in 1925 Brangwyn had worked unceasingly on the seventeen large panels, after preliminary work on quarter-size cartoons and innumerable studies in different media for figures, birds, animals and plants. Brangwyn was a superb draughtsman in a tradition already beginning to be discredited in the late twenties. The drawings in red, blue and black crayon of animals and plants are masterly in execution and in quality superior to the finished panels. These were treated in the manner of verdure tapestries, the colouring clear and bright, the subjects depicted with the minimum of shadows and sparely modelled in colour. The difference in scale of the various elements— figures peering through thickets of brightly coloured flowers nearly as large as themselves—gives some of the panels a curious and obviously unintended resemblance to Richard Dadd's *The Fairy Feller's Master Stroke*, where the tiny fantastic figures are similarly dwarfed by the surrounding vegetation. This riot of bright colour and the occasional illogicalities in the design probably influenced the Commission in their decision when they saw five of the panels erected in the gallery for which they were intended—a gallery noted for the gloomy melancholy of its decorations. Another factor which may have influenced them is that there was hardly any sky to be seen in any of the panels and, as any art dealer will witness, it is almost impossible to dispose of a landscape painting, no matter how exquisitely painted, which does not show at least a third of the canvas area as sky—an illogical reaction on the part of the picture-buying public, which keeps many restorers busy rearranging old paintings of views.

Brangwyn was not allowed to suffer financially by the rejection. The commission was honoured by Lord Iveagh's heir, and he finished the remaining panels, though with an inevitable sense of discouragement and the knowledge that, at the time, there was no home for them. An offer of £40,000 for the finished panels from an American admirer of Brangwyn was not his to accept. It is recorded that Brangwyn never saw the panels as an ensemble, though they were exhibited at the Daily Mail Ideal Home Exhibition in 1933. Eventually they were used as decorations for the new Guildhall at Swansea in Wales, and were unveiled by Prince George in 1934.

Possibly as a relaxation from his work on these panels, Brangwyn had found time to design a number of furnished rooms for an exhibition at Pollard and Sons which was opened by a fellow Academician, the portait painter Sir John Lavery, in October 1930. The furniture was made to his designs by Pollard's, the pottery, glass and carpets by Doulton, Powell, and Templeton respectively. Again the reception by the critics was lukewarm—even embarrassed—and that of a writer in *The Architectural Review* confirms the memories of the present writer: "Now quaint, now just a little art nouveau, now faintly reminiscent of this period or that, now 'modern' yet somehow not 'modern'." Obviously out of sympathy with the starkness of Modernism, Brangwyn seems to have attempted to establish a style with no affinities with any period, rather in the way that a designer faced with the problem of creating a setting for a play in, say, Atlantis or some other mythical milieu invents an idiom of decoration which he hopes has an air of authority but is nevertheless unconsciously flavoured by references to known periods.

Brangwyn's murals painted on silver leaf for the dining room of the *Empress of Britain* sank into the obscurity which usually seems to overwhelm the decorations on liners, while his murals in the Great Hall of the RCA Building in the Rockefeller Centre, New York, dating from 1934, were overshadowed by those of José-Maria Sert and of Diego Rivera, described by a contemporary as "the Raphael of Communism".

REX WHISTLER

Rex Whistler was twenty and fresh from the Slade School, where he had studied under Henry Tonks, when he was commissioned by Lord Duveen to decorate with mural paintings the restaurant of the Tate Gallery, a work which occupied him for two years. These paintings—still in the sketch state in one or two places, notably in the areas around the windows —were on the theme of "In Pursuit of Rare Meats" and demonstrate Whistler's admiration for the architecture of Inigo Jones and his eighteenth-century followers. A guide to the events depicted in the murals was written by Rex Whistler and Edith Olivier and later published as a pamphlet by the Trustees of the Tate Gallery. In this, various people and places depicted are referred to with anagrammatic titles: Tonks as Dr Knots, Pugin as Ugpin, and Bernard Shaw, who opened the room in 1927, as Count Brendar Wahs, "the Palace Librarian and Public Orator". These murals established the reputation of Whistler as a decorative artist and his wittily elegant designs were in great demand until his untimely death in 1944 at the age of thirty-nine.

Rex Whistler's art was sometimes dismissed as pastiche and nothing more, but this is less than the truth. There was no element intended to deceive, no deliberate imitation of the work of any one artist, but rather a synthesis of all the eighteenth-century draughtsmen. Most of his work incorporated decorative motifs from the late seventeenth century, though he was equally adept at conveying the precise atmosphere of the Regency, Victorian and Edwardian periods—and he drew in the mannered fashion because it came naturally and expressed his ideas as no other way could. The contemporary scene he avoided, with few exceptions: he made a small number of fashion drawings for *Vogue* and, at the time of the coronation of George VI and Queen Elizabeth, some portrait drawings of the King and Queen and princesses in their robes—and these, though skilled, give the impression of a certain lack of interest.

Whistler's many patrons were drawn from those whose tastes were more traditional than *avant-garde*. Living mainly in eighteenth-century houses, either inherited or acquired from choice, and surrounded by furniture and objects of the same date, they were people of cultivated, literary tastes. They might understand and even admire the latest developments in the decorative arts but preferred for their own surroundings the more serene products of the past. For them he tirelessly painted murals, drew bookplates, illustrated novels and volumes of poems. Through their patronage his work was brought to the attention of theatrical impresarios who had connections with this circle, and as a result theatregoers were given the benefit of some of the most beautiful productions of the thirties. Posters for the London Museum, the Tate Gallery and

Right: Part of Rex Whistler's murals at Port Lympne, Kent, home of Sir Philip Sassoon; the artist's fee was £800.

Below: The dining room at Plas Newydd, Gwynedd, painted by Rex Whistler for Lord Anglesey in 1937.

the London Underground enlivened the streets with his elegant wit.

Whistler's most important commission was for the dining room at Plas Newydd, the residence of Lord Anglesey. The long room, perhaps too long for its width, was transformed into a baroque loggia. The ceiling was coffered in *trompe l'œil*, the smaller walls at each end were treated architecturally with pilasters enclosing the chimney piece, and there were *œil de bœuf* grilles over the doors and false perspectives. The long wall facing the windows was transformed into a romantic, idealized landscape of a harbour surrounded by mountain ranges—a harbour dotted with islands reminiscent of Isola Bella, and crowded with

sailing vessels anchored in safety behind moles and jetties from the storm hinted at by the high-piled threatening clouds. Separating this landscape from the room and acting as a link between the real and the imaginary were low walls and a jetty littered with fishing tackle, anchors, chains and objects emblematic of the sea, while the painter's sense of humour, never for long absent, showed itself in a trident, wreathed in seaweed, propped against a classical urn, and a wet footprint on the pavement, with the implication that

Rex Whistler and the staircase mural he painted for Mrs Ewan Wallace in Hill Street, London, in 1930–31.

Costume design by Rex Whistler for the part of Ceres in the masque from *The Tempest*, produced at Stratford-upon-Avon in 1934.

Neptune had risen from the sea and was exploring this house which encroached on his domain. The treatment of the architectural details is masterly enough to satisfy the most scholarly enthusiast of the eighteenth century.

Rather different in treatment were the mural decorations at Brook House executed for Lord and Lady Louis Mountbatten. These were in the sitting room of the penthouse apartment of the block erected on the site of the former Brook House in Park Lane, and in this case the walls were treated as panels in three tiers, each panel enclosing a painted landscape, a trophy, a *trompe l'œil* alcove with a statue or an

allegorical composition. The criticism might be made that the over-all effect is crowded and restless, that there are too many vignettes, but the *grisaille* colouring and the quality of the paintings go far to mitigate this possible fault. The murals at Mottisfont Abbey, an essay in the eighteenth-century Gothic manner, are perhaps a trifle mechanical and betray the effect of numerous rejections of proposed designs—much of the repeated architectural detail was done by an assistant under the artist's supervision.

In 1930 The Cresset Press published an edition of *Gulliver's Travels* in two volumes with illustrations by Rex Whistler, an edition which has become a collector's item as only 195 copies on hand-made paper were produced. A surviving proof with Whistler's corrections shows the painstaking care he took to ensure that his illustrations were reproduced with complete fidelity and here again is demonstrated that passion for eighteenth-century architecture which was so characteristic. At first sight some of the architectural fantasies appear improbable, but on closer examination they prove to be entirely practical and could in fact be realized in stone and brick. The success of this edition led to Whistler's work being in demand for other illustrations, notably for *The Lord Fish* by Walter de la Mare, *Fairy Tales and Legends* by Hans Andersen, *The Next Volume* by Edward James and for the volume of poems *Armed October* by his brother Laurence Whistler. He designed dustjackets for Isaak Dinesen's *Seven Gothic Tales*, Constance Wright's *Silver Collar Boy*, Vincent Sheean's *San Felice* and for Laurence Whistler's definitive volume *Sir John Vanbrugh*, a study of an architect with whom, in versatility, Rex Whistler had much in common.

However, it was in his work for the theatre that Rex Whistler reached the widest public. Charles B. Cochran, always ready to encourage new talent, gave him his first opportunity—a small scene in Cochran's 1931 revue at the old London Pavilion Theatre in Piccadilly Circus. The Cochran revues and other productions which were so much a part of theatrical life in the 1930s were always mounted with taste and style and among the many decorative artists who were given an opportunity by Cochran was Christian Bérard, then unknown in England, again in the 1931 revue. From 1933 Whistler designed one or more productions for the theatre or the ballet practically every year. *Ballerina* in 1933, settings for *Fidelio* at Covent Garden in 1934 (settings worthy of revival), a *Marriage of Figaro* at Sadler's Wells and in 1935 the costumes and settings for the ballet *The Rake's Progress* inspired by Hogarth's engravings with the addition of a drop curtain representing a street in eighteenth-century London.

Nobody in the audience at Sadler's Wells witnessing the first performance of *The Wise Virgins*, a ballet with Whistler's designs, could possibly have imagined that the scenery and costumes would be destroyed through enemy action in Holland five years later in 1940 and that some of the dancers would barely escape with their lives. The backcloth depicted the baroque gates to heaven and the costumes of the frivolous foolish virgins left one breast bare—or seemingly so, for in the less permissive thirties what appeared to be bare flesh was actually chiffon with a rosy nipple painted on.

In 1935 *Victoria Regina* by Laurence Houseman was presented at the Broadhurst Theatre in New York with Rex Whistler's explorations into nineteenth-century styles. This play was presented with designs by Roger Furse in London at the tiny Gate Theatre —regulations regarding the portrayal of royalty meant it was not possible to admit the public, so that the London showing was limited to this club theatre. These regulations did not apply to New York, of course, where the Whistler designs, especially the scene in the tartan tent erected in the grounds of Balmoral, were widely admired; in the opinion of many, they were influential in furthering the popular revival of interest in Victoriana. In 1936 London saw a never-to-be-forgotten production of *Pride and Prejudice* with Whistler's charming scenery and costumes as a setting for the performance of Celia Johnson, the perfect embodiment of Elizabeth Bennett.

Almost archaeological in their attention to period detail but at the same time composed into beautiful stage pictures, Whistler's settings avoided any garish extravagance and his costumes were always exactly right for the character, without any eccentric and bizarre exaggerations of period characteristics.

DUNCAN GRANT

Duncan Grant was active during the thirties as a mural painter (often in conjunction with Vanessa Bell), as a designer of textiles, and as a designer of ceramics. He and Vanessa Bell created a music room, characteristic of their style, which was exhibited at Alex Reid and Lefevre Ltd in 1933. An illustration in colour of part of the room can be seen in *Colour Schemes for the Modern Home* by Derek Patmore and shows the carpets, fabrics, ornaments and tiled hearth decorated in their typical calligraphic style. The fabrics by Duncan Grant were printed by Allan Walton and incorporated a swagged border design which was used as a pelmet and on the upholstered settee and chairs.

MAYOR GALLERY

There are certain galleries whose closing leaves a gap that can never be quite filled. Usually the reflection of the individual taste of one or two people either indifferent to or independent of commercial stresses, they generate a quality of excitement, freshness and originality which sets them apart from the average commercial gallery. They show less interest in the current exhibitions than in the more profitable sale of paintings by established artists in regular stock. Curtis Moffat's shop and gallery must have been one such, as was the Arthur Jeffress gallery at a more recent date —both, incidentally, were run by Americans.

The Mayor Gallery in Cork Street, London, under proprietors Frederick Mayor and Douglas Cooper, introduced the work of many Continental artists to the British public—work which was met too often by a cool indifference. The gallery opened in April 1933, the frontage in a then shocking colour scheme of white, orange and vermilion. The interior was designed by Brian O'Rorke in a fashionably Mod-

Right: Wood panel painted in oils by Duncan Grant, 1933, which formed part of the decoration of a music room by Grant and Vanessa Bell in their characteristic calligraphic style. The designs were exhibited at the gallery of Alex Reid and Lefevre, London.

ernist scheme, the simplicity of which offered no competition to the exhibits, which was enhanced by pale blue walls and indirect lighting hidden by false hanging ceilings. Arundell Clarke designed the furniture. Here Paul Klee had his first exhibition in London (with extremely poor sales) and in the following year George Grosz was introduced to the British public. Max Ernst, Joan Miró, Edward Wadsworth, flower paintings by Marie Laurencin framed in wide bands of antique mirror (commissioned by Lady Cunard for her dining room in Grosvenor Square and presented with a catalogue foreword by Somerset Maugham), George Rouault, Aristide Maillol, Max Jacob, Christian Bérard, portrait drawings by Jean Cocteau (at 12 guineas each), Curtis Moffat photographs and Allan Walton fabrics—all these were among the exhibits at the Mayor Gallery between its inception and the outbreak of war. An early show in 1933 was that of Unit One, a group exhibition with works by Paul Nash, Ben Nicholson, Edward Wadsworth, Frances Hodgkins,

Henry Moore and Barbara Hepworth, the first exhibition to be gathered to illustrate an art book—*Art Now* by Herbert Read.

ETIENNE DRIAN

Drian's fashion drawings appeared in *Le Gazette du Bon Ton* in 1913 and during the twenties and thirties he drew in charcoal or sanguine most of the elegant women of the day. In addition to his portrait drawings, which were somewhat in the tradition of Boldini, he executed many decorative paintings and screens.

Versailles and its gardens had a particular appeal for him; the Cent Pas appear in the panels he executed for Elsie de Wolfe in the Villa Trianon at Versailles and again in the *trompe-l'œil* murals in an apartment decorated by Nasenta. Here views of Versailles in late eighteenth-century frames appear to be held up by asymmetrical arrangements of cords and are partially obscured by swags and draperies, equally simulated.

EMILIO TERRY

Terry, one of the most imaginative architect-designers of the thirties, collaborated with George Balanchine in the scenario for the ballet *Les Valses de Beethoven* which was part of the repertory of Les Ballets 1933. The story, a version of the myth of Apollo and Daphne, was less remarkable than the decor and settings. Terry later worked with Carlos de Beistegui in creating with exquisite taste a series of interior decorations and follies.

THE NEO-ROMANTICS

Christian Bérard, Pavel Tchelitchew, the brothers Eugène and Léonid Berman, Thérèse Desbaines and Kristians Tonny formed the group known as the "Neo-Romantics" when they first exhibited at the Galerie Druet. There is a curious lack of agreement as to the date of this exhibition. Waldemar George, writing in 1934 and giving the group an alternative title of "Neo-Humanists", gives a date of 1924; Julien Levy

Painted screen by Etienne Drian, about 1938.

Settings by Emilio Terry for *Les Valses de Beethoven*, 1933.

places it in 1925, while Lincoln Kirstein in his monograph on the drawings of Pavel Tchelitchew gives yet another date, 1926, a date confirmed by Parker Tyler in his recent biography of Tchelitchew. Even the spelling of the name of the gallery varies between Druet and Drouot. All the members of the group had studied at the Académie Ranson where they had been influenced by Maurice Denis, Vuillard, Bonnard and Valloton. Desbaines, of whom little was heard after that first exhibition, and Bérard were French, and Tonny was Danish. The others were Russian, and all three had spent years since their leaving Russia during the Revolution in wandering from one country to another, studying under different masters, before settling in Paris. These years, with their different influences, left their mark in characteristics which were to become more pronounced in time, though at the point when their ways coincided and for a brief period they could be collectively designated as Neo-Romantics. All of them were under the spell of Picasso's Blue Period with, in the opinion of Waldemar George, traces of Cubism, Expressionism, Surrealism and the imagery of popular art.

EUGÈNE BERMAN

Eugène Berman's sojourns in Rome and Venice had imbued him with an enthusiasm for Palladian, Mannerist and baroque architecture which became the predominating factor in his paintings, murals and stage designs. The melancholy of ruined architecture took precedence over the human condition as subject-matter in his compositions and he coupled this with an absorption in the ingenuities of *trompe l'œil*. Figures, when incorporated into the compositions of ruined, crumbling architecture, invariably represented beggars or gipsies, dispossessed and wandering, introduced less as individuals than as devices to give scale to the architecture or to accentuate the desolate melancholy of the scene. The bizarre landscape of Les Baux, with its weather-worn rocks tortured into freakish shapes, appears many times as a setting for decayed architectural vistas under skies filled with perspectives of fleecy clouds, vistas depicting the aftermath of a titanic struggle between rocks, trees and buildings.

Berman's paintings earned him the patronage of a number of distinguished collectors during the 1930s. Arthur Jeffress, already the owner of a number of canvases by de Chirico, whose use of architectural perspectives to give a surreal effect of a disturbing sense of strangeness had been an early influence on Berman, became an enthusiastic collector of Berman's paintings. He created a setting for them, in collaboration with John Hill of Green and Abbott, of Empire furniture and sombre walls and curtains in shades of tobacco brown and spinach green in the dining room of his country house near Winchester. Edward James acquired a number of Berman's paintings and drawings. A trip to America in 1935 enlarged Berman's circle of admirers and the scope of his activities. For Julien Levy, author of a volume devoted to Berman's work from the early exhibitions in Paris during the twenties until the mid forties, he executed a series of mural paintings in *trompe l'œil*, depicting meticulously detailed empty picture frames apparently riddled with age and worm-holes, inlaid in a chevron design of

Left: Eugène Berman photographed in Paris in about 1938 by Peter Rose Pulham, one of series of portraits of artists taken for *Harper's Bazaar*.

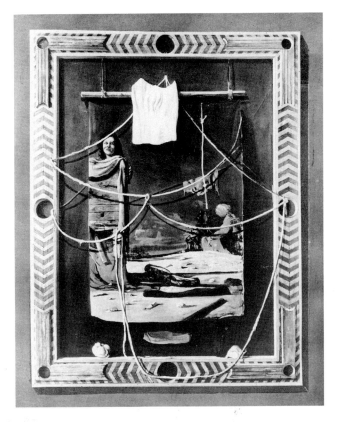

Trompe l'œil panel by Eugène Berman, one of a series painted in 1936 for Julien Levy.

differently coloured woods. In lieu of pictures they enclosed painted representations of tattered scraps of canvas, some depicting scenes of gipsy encampments, scraps of drapery, pebbles or sprouting bulbs criss-crossed and, as it were, trapped in a fragile cage of knotted strings which cast their painted shadows on the objects behind them. The walls of the room itself were painted in exactly the same colour as that of the backgrounds of the panels in order to accentuate the deception.

In the same year, 1936, he completed a series of painted panels of beggars and their makeshift tents of tattered draperies for the dining room of James Thrall Sobey and in 1938, in a room for Wright Ludington, he experimented further in illusionistic techniques. Here the wrinkled and torn canvas with scenes of desolate landscapes with figures is apparently carefully pinned to the wall, framed by and superimposed upon still more ragged fabric.

Berman's poetic obsession with fantastic architecture and its treatment in perspective, combined with his faculty for conveying a disturbing atmosphere of still, magical desolation, rendered him particularly eligible for designing for the theatre and, in particular, for ballet. But apart from a number of projects which never came to fruition his only stage work of note during the thirties consisted of settings and costumes for the ballet *The Devil's Holiday* presented in 1939 by the Ballets Russes de Monte Carlo with choreography by Frederick Ashton to music by Niccolo Paganini. Berman designed several covers for the periodical *Town and Country* before the war but his most frequent contributions in this field, as in ballet, were executed after 1940.

A painted wardrobe exhibited at the newly opened Galerie Drouin a month or so before the outbreak of war shows what Eugène Berman might have accomplished if given the opportunities to realize his architectural fantasies in three dimensions. In this piece of decorative furniture he achieved, by forcing illusionistic techniques of painting to their utmost limit, the effect of a ruined stone framework—built perversely as a ruin, opening on to the limpid sky with no horizon and punctuated by bronze rings which serve no purpose, nails and odd pieces of wood and rags, which by the simplest means contribute to as great a feeling of strangeness as all of the sometimes strained imagery of Salvador Dali.

LÉONOR FINI

An early exhibition of Léonor Fini's paintings in 1934 had attracted the favourable notice of the critic German Bazin and, although the painter's name was misspelt as "Chini", the terms used to describe her ("elle a presque un air de suffragette") and her work ("hermaphroditism, auto-eroticism, sapphism . . . equivocal") were enough to intrigue a new circle of admirers.

GALERIE DROUIN

The Galerie Drouin, specializing in the work of leading Surrealist and Neo-Romantic painters, was opened in

Above: Decorative panels by Léonor Fini, shown at the Galerie Drouin, Paris, in 1939.

Left: Trompe l'œil wardrobe painted by Eugène Berman and first exhibited at the Galerie Drouin, Paris, in 1939.

the Place Vendôme in the summer of 1939. Everything seemed favourable for its success, the decorations were lavish, the site excellent (next to the Schiaparelli boutique), the painters exhibiting had considerable reputations—only the opening date was ill omened. The decorations of the three main rooms were remarkable, for each was devoted to a single colour—grey, sapphire blue and red. The walls, including the mouldings, were covered in velvet with the carpet exactly matching, the early eighteenth-century ceilings being painted white. Each room took on the semblance of a precious casket enshrining the paintings displayed and the sole exhibit in the red room was a large and sinister canvas by Max Ernst. Among the other exhibits was the *trompe l'œil* cupboard by Eugène Berman and another painted by Léonor Fini with winged seraphim.

CHRISTIAN BÉRARD

The years of the Depression had not allowed many opportunities for elegance or gaiety. By 1934, however, there were signs of recovery which coincided with the appearance in the pages of *Vogue* of drawings by an artist new to the majority of the magazine readers, though his reputation had been steadily growing among the cognoscenti of Paris since the Galerie Druet exhibition ten years before. This artist, Christian Bérard, was to wield a growing influence on taste in the theatre, fashion and decoration—he was in many ways to occupy the position formerly held by Paul Poiret.

Christian Bérard's work had attracted the favourable attention of the influential critic Gustave Geffroy some time before the Galerie Druet exhibition which added so considerably to his reputation as a painter. Waldemar George, the artistic editor of *L'Amour de l'Art*, became another enthusiastic supporter, writing articles on Bérard's work and giving high praise in particular to his portraits which he considered reflected the painter's admiration for Fayum funerary portraits. Other critics praised Bérard's "désir d'exprimer la vie intérieure" and drew flattering parallels with Degas—no small compliment to a painter still in his twenties. Waldemar George's support was unfailing. When a series of panels painted by Bérard with reminiscences of Le Nain were commissioned by the architect Pierre Barbe and then refused, George rushed to the painter's defence, declaring in print that such a refusal was nothing but an honour for Bérard.

Bérard was criticized during his lifetime for neglecting his more serious painting in favour of fashionable but less permanent pursuits. It is possible that he found a greater outlet for his fertile imagination in magazine covers and fashion drawings and in designs for the theatre and in particular for the ballet. Certainly as a result of them he became the virtual arbiter of taste in Paris during the second half of the thirties. Few designers have had so many opportunities of disseminating their work. Hardly an issue of *Vogue* appeared without a contribution from him in some form or another, whether a cover, a series of fashion drawings in colour, or illustrations to a feature article on fashion

or decoration, and his decors and costumes for the Ballets Russes were seen by audiences in the United States and South America as the company went on their lengthy tours.

Yet of this enormous body of work little remains to record the achievement of perhaps the most influential designer of the thirties. None of the ballets he designed is still in the repertory of any company. Copies of *Vogue* or of any periodical to which he contributed, either during the thirties or in the post-war years, are extremely scarce. The setting and the lovely clothes for *Cotillon*, for *Symphonie Fantastique* or *Septième Symphonie*, for the plays *La Voix Humaine* and *La Machine Infernale* by Jean Cocteau, for *La Reine Margot* and *Cyrano de Bergerac*—all of these survive only in memories, or in photographs which fail to convey the magic of the originals. Bérard's draughtsmanship, apparently effortless and at times reminiscent of Japanese drawings, was combined with a highly personal use of colours associated with the fairgrounds and circuses which he depicted so often and with such sympathy—the brilliant pastel shades of clowns' costumes, candy floss and cheap sweets, the deep rich crimson of velvet theatre-curtains or the

Left: Christian Bérard, photographed in Paris in about 1938 by Peter Rose Pulham.

Above: "The Hand of Fate" dance from the ballet *Cotillon*, with settings and costumes designed by Bérard, 1932. The dancers were Lubov Rostova and David Lichine.

Right: Design for *La Septième Symphonie* by Christian Bérard, first performed by the Ballets Russes de Monte Carlo on 5 May 1936.

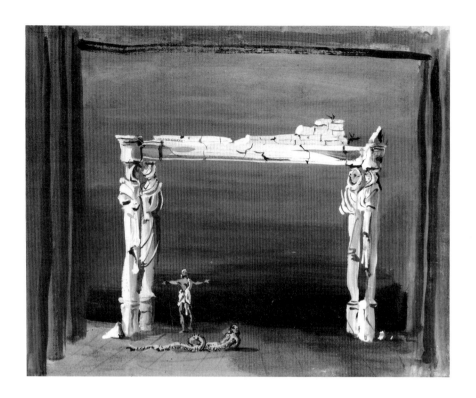

Left: The *pas de deux* from *La Symphonie Fantastique,* designed by Christian Bérard for the Ballets Russes de Monte Carlo in 1936. The choreography was by Léonide Massine to music by Berlioz.

Below: Design by Christian Bérard for the ballroom scene in *La Symphonie Fantastique.* The blood-red arcades giving on to a view of a desert with a brooding winged sphinx provided a perfect setting for the feverish mood of the symphony's second movement, and set in relief the whirling figures of the dancers in their romantic white dresses (though at the Covent Garden premiere one or two of the dresses showed a slight tendency to fall apart).

violets and deep greens of grapes, moss and ivy. With a few strokes of a brush he could draw on his knowledge of architecture to suggest a period, and his fashion drawings, economical to the point of leaving out the faces entirely, transmute the models into a timeless elegance, however typical of the style of a certain year. It is difficult to overestimate Bérard's influence on taste in Paris and elsewhere, for his advice and approval were sought by dressmakers, interior decorators and leaders of fashion.

MME KARINSKA

Bérard's costume designs, like his fashion drawings in *Vogue*, were evocative rather than explicit and, in the hands of an ordinary dressmaker, their magic could have been blunted. Together with other painters working in the theatre he was fortunate in having his sketches interpreted with great sensitivity by Mme Karinska who, with creative artistry of a high degree, was able to translate Bérard's calligraphic doodles into practical clothes that worked in a feasible manner and, at the same time, retained the intangible feeling of the original drawing. Her unorthodox dressmaking could transform a scarf or sash, rendered in an apparently hurried and careless manner by Bérard with a brush-stroke or two of Chinese white, into a drapery which was a replica of the original in movement and in repose.

Mme Karinska's methods of interpretation were as unconventional as her life prior to her first theatrical commission, the making of Derain's costumes for the ballet *Concurrence* in 1932. No one at the ecstatic premiere of Massine's ballet *Symphonie Fantastique* would have found it easy to believe that the creator of Bérard's lovely costumes in the ballroom scene had been, not so long before, the editor of a socialist newspaper in Russia. She and her first husband (Karinsky was her second husband) were extremely politically minded before and during the Bolshevik Revolution, but with the changing temperature of political thought in Russia she judged it expedient, on being offered an important museum appointment, to declare it necessary to study museum techniques in Germany. On being given official permission to do so she left Russia never to return. Her artistic inclinations

had led her to apply for tuition in painting to Sovely Sorine, who coldly refused, though he later admitted that he had been wrong.

Her introduction to the theatre came about, it was reported, as a result of repairing the ballet dress of a dancer, a fellow exile from Russia. She did this with so much skill that, much to her relief as she was extremely hard up, more important tasks were entrusted to her talents. Apart from her collaboration with Bérard, she and the couturier Agnès made the costumes for a production of *The Cenci* starring the beautiful Ilya Abdy and, surprisingly, designed by Balthus: as a result, the Renaissance berets and doublets featured in the play had a considerable influence on the Paris collections of 1935. She realized the designs of Raoul Dufy for *Beach*, a charming lightweight ballet which failed to survive more than a season or two after its premiere in 1933. Also in 1935, she worked with Jean Hugo on the designs for *Les Cent Baisers*, an underrated ballet with music by Jean Françaix and choreography by Bronislava Nijinska. Hugo's witty allusions to the lithographic illustrations in nineteenth-century books of fairy tales failed to gain the appreciation the designs deserved and objections were made that the heroine, danced by Irina Baronova, was dressed in black. Karinska also worked with Cassandre who, by a coincidence, was born of French parents in Karkov, the town where Karinska and her first husband had pursued their editorial careers.

PAVEL TCHELITCHEW

Pavel Tchelitchew, like Berman and Bérard, was drawn into the milieu of the ballet soon after the exhibition at the Galerie Druet and was the only one to work in direct contact with Serge Diaghilev. *Ode*, designed in 1928, was Massine's last ballet for Diaghilev and, despite the latter's straining after novelty to keep the attention of the public, he seems to have taken little interest in the production. Tchelitchew in his decors indicated the preoccupations with metaphysics and hermetic mysteries which were later to confuse and even alienate his admirers, and the complications of the settings, with rows of dolls in perspective suspended on a network of cords, film projections and illuminated costumes, were too much

Tchelitchew

of a novelty even for Diaghilev. Edward James embraced the work of Tchelitchew as much as that of Berman and Bérard and, in addition to collecting some of the painter's best early drawings and canvases, he commissioned Tchelitchew to design the ballet *Errante* for Les Ballets 1933, organized by James to further the career of his wife Tilly Losch. Tchelitchew was at the time working on the theme of draperies in metamorphic compositions and for the ballet he devised a setting composed of white draperies. Arnold Haskell, already assuming the mantle of high priest of the ballet, described the scenery as "a big white sale" and made scathing comments about Tilly Losch's dress with its train thirty feet (nine metres) long. One of the rooms in Edward James's London house was strongly reminiscent of the setting for this ballet.

Several important paintings by Tchelitchew were hung in a decor of festooned draperies supported by marble columns and a marble Renaissance mantelpiece which had come from Lord Rosebery's collection. And the decors of *Errante* were possibly the original inspiration for the plaster draperies used by a number of decorators in London and Paris during the thirties. The process of making these plaster draperies was both difficult and messy as the required pieces of fabric had to be soaked in liquid plaster and placed in position in a matter of moments before the plaster set hard. No second thoughts or alterations were possible so that in most cases it served as a simple form of tenting—it was useful for disguising awkward corners—or in simple swags draped over a pole for the pelmets in a Regency scheme. Usually the effect desired was in the romantic baroque vein but no attempts were made to emulate the fantasy of the baroque ceiling of the ballroom in the Palazzo Albrizzi in Venice, dating from 1712, with its elaborate agitated draperies upheld by flying cherubs.

In 1935 Tchelitchew designed *Nobilissime Visione*, a ballet based on the life of St Francis of Assisi, choreographed by Massine for the Ballets de Monte Carlo.

Left: Pavel Tchelitchew, photographed by Cecil Beaton in 1935 in front of a large painting, spangled with sequins, which was commissioned by the Prince Matchabelli and used by Beaton as a backdrop to a series of fashion photographs for *Vogue* in 1935.

GERMAN DECORATIVE PICTURES

Significant of the times and the prevailing influence in Germany is the type of painting or decorative picture to be found in the rooms featured in decorating magazines during the 1930s and particularly after 1933. A careful examination of a periodical such as *Innen Dekoration* will show that, in photographs of interiors, the paintings are such that there could be no possibility of the owner being accused of harbouring decadent art. Possibly anyone owning a picture by a proscribed artist would have discreetly removed it and replaced it with a harmless substitute before the photograph was taken, knowing that the magazine was likely to be scrutinized closely and any offender denounced—though it is more likely that to avoid denunciation, even by a member of the family, a controversial painting would have been disposed of in any case.

A necessarily anonymous correspondent to *The Studio* gives a revealing picture of the state of affairs in artistic circles in Germany in 1935, two years after the seizure of power by Adolf Hitler. An annual exhibition in Munich totalling 820 paintings, drawings and etchings closed with a total of 182 sold, of which just over half were acquired by the state. The cash value of the exhibits sold was considerably lower than in previous years. This was the first exhibition fully to show the effects of the new compulsory registration by every artist at the Chamber of Culture, a body with leaders appointed by Dr Goebbels. Included in the exhibits were five bronze busts of Hitler "in the familiar defiant posture" (he had not posed for any of them); a painting of two Hitler youths learning to play the flute from an old village musician, bought by Baldur von Shirach, the head of the Hitler Youth Organization; and a view of a village decorated for the elections of 1933 which was purchased by the Ministry of Propaganda, giving rise to the comment in the article that "it is fairly safe to assert that such a picture with the words 'Wir Wollen den Frieden' flaunted on bunting in the foreground would not have met with the aesthetic approval of a pre-Hitler jury."

7

THE SURREALIST INFLUENCE ON DECORATION

or many people the Surrealist Exhibition which opened in June 1936 at the New Burlington Galleries in London was the first opportunity of seeing the work of a movement which had its inception before the First World War.

A few painters, poets and writers in England were familiar with the somewhat vague philosophies behind the Surrealist movement, which was regarded in some quarters with suspicion because of its shifting political associations. A few patrons, Edward James for instance, wisely purchased some of the best early work of Dali, Magritte, Picabia and other painters who were attempting to realize Rimbaud's philosophy that life must be changed by depicting the workings of the subconscious mind. Films made by Salvador Dali and Luis Buñuel, *Un Chien Andalou* and *L'Age d'Or*, had had an extremely limited showing in private cinema clubs since they were made in 1929 and 1930 respectively, but the circuit managers would not have allowed either of them, even if the local authorities permitted their being shown, to disturb or alienate a public accustomed to Al Jolson or Shirley Temple. Similarly, the periodical *Minotaure*, founded in 1933

Left: "Mae West" by Salvador Dali, 1934, a design for an anthropomorphic interior for Edward James. For details of the "mouth" settee, see page 176.

Below: "The Phantom of Sex Appeal", a metamorphic sculptural composition shown at the 1936 exhibition, photographed by Bill Brandt.

Left: "Object (Le Déjeuner en fourrure)" by Meret Oppenheim, shown at the Surrealist Exhibition in London, 1936.

Below left: Max Ernst beside a mannequin in the "Rue Surréaliste" in the Surrealist Exhibition in Paris, 1938, photographed by Peter Rose Pulham.

Below: "Water", wood engraving by Max Ernst for *Une Semaine de Bonté, ou les Sept Elements Capitaux*, 1934.

and enlivened with cover designs by Picasso, Derain, Miró, Ernst, Magritte, Dali and Duchamp, was obtainable only in one or two bookshops in London, where its high price and French text ensured the smallest circulation. The general public were unprepared for the impact of this, the first international exhibition of Surrealism. The press, delighted to have an opportunity of being facetious at the expense of other artists besides Jacob Epstein and Pablo Picasso, their usual targets, seized every occasion to express horror and indignation at the many exhibits. One in particular, the tea-cup, saucer and spoon made of squirrel fur by Meret Oppenheim, became almost a symbol of the whole exhibition. Every day for the two weeks the show lasted the galleries were crowded with visitors, most of whom came to jeer or to be shocked. Many, however, were won over by the gaiety and impudent wit of certain of the exhibits—not all of them of uniform quality, it must be admitted—and the more perceptive realized the sincerity and importance of the movement.

The organizer of the exhibition was the English painter and collector Roland Penrose and through his initiative the work of more than sixty artists from fourteen countries was shown collectively for the first time. In addition there were Surrealist *objets trouvés*, drawings by children and the mentally disturbed, sculpture and objects from Africa, Oceania and America—such a diverse collection of apparently unrelated artefacts that some members of the public began to feel uneasy at the thought of so much "surrealism" having been in their lives without their realizing it. The following December an even larger exhibition was organized by Alfred Barr in New York under the title "Fantastic Art, Dada and Surrealism". In this case the boundaries of Surrealism, already extensive, were enlarged to include the work of artists and designers of the past—Dürer, Bosch, Arcimboldo, Piranesi, Hogarth and many others. The catalogue ran to 250 pages. Again the press and the critics alternated between abuse and praise. Before the exhibition left for a tour of a number of cities in America, attempts were made to impose censorship by removing some exhibits which were considered too shocking—the fur tea-cup and saucer was one—but this move was

defeated and the exhibition toured in its entirety.

Both these exhibitions could be regarded as dress rehearsals for that held in Paris early in 1938. Far more ambitiously conceived and with the purpose of avoiding any atmosphere of a museum or gallery, this took the form of tableaux and theatrical set pieces. Salvador Dali's "Taxi Pluvieux" with its snail-encrusted occupant continually drenched in rain; the "Rue Surréaliste" inhabited by mannequins designed by Man Ray, Max Ernst, Dali, Yves Tanguy, Marcel Duchamp and others; an enormous room with beds, pools of water, ferns and a ceiling hung with hundreds of sacks

Marcel Duchamp beneath the ceiling hung with sacks of coal at the 1938 exhibition, photographed by Peter Rose Pulham.

Left: Settee in the shape of Mae West's lips, designed by Salvador Dali; covered in deep pink and pale pink felt, it was made for Edward James by Green & Abbott of Wigmore Street, London, in about 1936. Five versions were ordered, in London and from Jean-Michel Frank in Paris; two, in shocking pink satin, were intended for Schiaparelli's London salon, but she changed her mind and they were never delivered.

of coal by Marcel Duchamp—these were only a few of the fantasies assembled to shock and delight.

It is obvious that these exhibitions contributed enormously to the general taste for fantasy which was current from the mid thirties until the outbreak of war. Designers, decorators, commercial artists, dressmakers, jewellers and photographers strained their imaginations to the utmost to produce fantasies in the Surrealist vein. The more decorative aspects of the movement were cultivated and the sinister, violent and macabre avoided or at least alluded to only obliquely.

The exhibitions, particularly those in New York and Paris, had shown that elements of Surrealism could be found in most periods of the past from the sixteenth century onwards and the strong flavour of the nineteenth century which could be seen in many contemporary Surrealist creations—for example, Max Ernst's collages of Victorian prints, in which illustrations of that period were rearranged with malevolent results—provided a link with the current revival of Victoriana.

The Vicomte and Vicomtesse de Noailles were ardent patrons of painters, poets and musicians and their salon, decorated by Jean-Michel Frank, was the meeting place of fashion and the arts. They had financed the making of the *avant-garde* films *L'Age*

d'Or and *Le Sang d'un Poète*. The Vicomtesse, under the name "Marie-Laure", had exhibitions as a painter and is often mentioned in publications of the thirties as an exponent of Surrealism.

Among the most fantastic examples of Surrealism in the decorative arts were Schiaparelli's creations. Schiaparelli had sought the advice of Jean-Michel Frank concerning the decoration of her various apartments, and for her Frank used Dali's design for a pink settee in the shape of Mae West's lips, derived from several drawings representing the actress as a room, her nostrils forming a fireplace, her eyes two framed pictures and her hair the swirling looped draperies or *portières*.

THE APARTMENT OF CARLOS DE BEISTEGUI

In 1936 *The Architectural Review* featured an apartment in Paris which combined a certain Surrealist perverseness with extreme luxury—all the more surprising as the austere surroundings designed by Le Corbusier were a setting for nineteenth-century mock-baroque of an exuberance completely alien to the ideals of an architect who maintained that a house was a machine for living in. The explanation of this anomaly was given a year or two later by Jean-Michel Frank. Between the time that the work on the structure of the penthouse had finished and the moment when it was necessary to decide on the furnishings, Modernism had become as "démodé as Art Nouveau" and consequently a more exuberant and decorative style was imposed upon Le Corbusier's austerity.

Carlos de Beistegui was then on the threshold of a career as one of the great patrons of the decorative arts in this century. A privately printed volume of his own poems, *Songeries*, illustrated with coloured reproductions of his drawings, very much in the Paul Poiret–George Barbier manner, had marked his debut

as a patron as far back as 1914, but the decorations of the penthouse overlooking the Etoile were very different from the derivative "Persian" of his earlier enthusiasm. Le Corbusier's structure was simplicity itself —an arrangement of stark, unornamented boxes with huge plate-glass windows, terraces and roof gardens on several levels. Consisting of a salon, dining room, bedroom, bathroom and kitchen, it was a machine for entertaining. At a touch of a button, entire walls appeared or disappeared, windows slid back to incorporate terrace into room, chandeliers slid along hidden rails in the ceiling to allow uninterrupted screening of movies projected from apertures ordinarily concealed behind ormulu wall brackets superimposed on framed mirrors. The use of electricity was confined to the elaborate mechanical tricks in the apartment, for the only illumination was from candles

Drawing room in the Paris apartment of Carlos de Beistegui, early 1930s.

Left: The roof garden of Carlos de Beistegui's Paris aparment, early 1930s. The lawn was finely kept and sprinkled with daisies, and set against the wall were pieces of imitation furniture and a fireplace made of stone.

Left: Drawing room in Carlos de Beistegui's apartment, early 1930s. The framed mirrors with their superimposed candle sconces slid to one side at the touch of a button to reveal film projectors. The spiral staircase led to the roof garden and the only illumination was from candles.

whose flattering light was reflected from the white walls and ceiling of the salon to shine softly on the glass chairs, the white and gold rococo commode and the ice-blue velvet of the curtains and upholstery of the Second Empire white and gold settees and on the *pièce de résistance* of the decor—an over-life-size figure of a blackamoor dressed in ostrich feathers and standing on a white and gold rococo pedestal. This had been specially made to the order of Beistegui in Dresden porcelain and was inspired by the smaller eighteenth-century porcelain figures which decorated the dining table and were reflected in the panelled mirror doors.

But the ultimate fantasy was to be found in the

roof garden where a magnificent eighteenth-century portrait was casually hung on an outside wall, where entire box hedges slid apart to reveal views of Paris, and where one finally arrived at an open-air room. The floor was carpeted with a daisy-strewn lawn, there were a fireplace with a clock, candlesticks surmounted by a circular picture which was actually a view of the Arc de Triomphe, and a marble "commode" supporting a birdcage with a mechanical songster.

EDWARD JAMES

Edward James in his novel *The Gardener who saw God*, published in 1937, depicted an English nobleman of great fortune whose passion for Surrealism finally

Edward James at his desk in the "tent" room in Wimpole Street, photographed in 1936 by Norman Parkinson.

Left: Cover for a telephone receiver in the form of a lobster, designed by Salvador Dali for Edward James in 1936, and used in James's house in Wimpole Street.

Right: Table by Costa-Achillopulo with a glass top on a carved wood and plaster base, about 1935.

Below right: Ceramic teapot with Surrealist hand motifs from the collection of Edward James, late 1930s.

ruined him. Always conventionally dressed, with the exception of a gold and enamel tiepin made to represent a tiny poached egg, such was his passion for the work of the Surrealists in general and Salvador Dali in particular that his Gothic castle in Berkshire was surrounded by marble grand pianos hoisted into trees, colossal poached eggs of painted alabaster apparently floating in the pools, dovecotes made of sponges and a hen roost of cheese, while "two large Elizabethan yews which had formerly been chipped into the likeness of a lion and a unicorn . . . [were] now retrimmed into the shape of that pair of half-bowed, half-stooping figures of a French peasant and his wife at evening prayer taken from the well-known picture by Millet called 'The Angelus'." A loaf of real bread thirty-five yards (thirty-two metres) in length was placed on the lawn, thousands of painted porcelain imitations of ants and grasshoppers were spread under the beeches, sewing machines and umbrellas carved from granite served as garden seats. "The good, mad lord"

finally ruined himself by these extravagant follies, the finishing touch being the construction of two gigantic ears which he built on to the north and south wings of his home, ears large enough to contain sitting rooms, electric organs and a Turkish bath.

Almost as strange were the decorations of Edward James's own houses at 35 Wimpole Street, London, and in Sussex. They included telephone receivers designed by Salvador Dali in the shape of lobsters.

SURREALIST FURNITURE, MOTIFS AND IMAGERY

Dali's "mouth" settee and Schiaparelli's bizarre buttons of red galalith representing lips were in the Surrealist tradition of Man Ray's celebrated painting eight feet (two and a half metres) long, "A l'Heure de L'Observatoire—Les Amoureux", in which "red lips

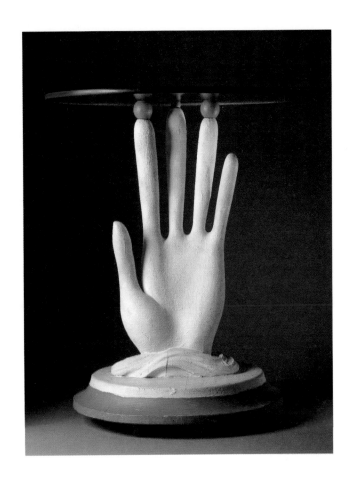

floated in a blueish-grey sky over a twilight landscape with an observatory and its two domes like breasts dimly indicated on the horizon". Equally Surrealist was Kurt Seligmann's "L'Ultra-Meuble", a stool made of four realistic legs wearing high-heeled shoes joined above the bent knees to form a stool—a combined piece of furniture and *objet fabriqué* exhibited in the Paris Surrealist Exhibition. Raoh Schorr, a Swiss sculptor working in London, had created a number of glass-topped tables supported by realistically modelled human legs for display purposes a year or two previously, and Costa-Achillopulo's table in the form of an over-scaled hand equally antedates "L'Ultra-Meuble" by at least three years.

This absorption during the thirties with portions of human anatomy as decorative objects concentrated even more upon the hand, and in this the trends of Surrealism and Victoriana found a motif in common. Man Ray, Max Ernst and Joyen had all at one time or another used the human hand, divorced from the

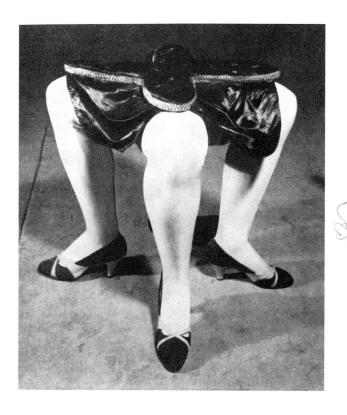

Constance Spry had brought once more into fashion. The life-size carved marble hands resting on realistically rendered books or cushions fashionable as keepsakes—Queen Victoria had all her children's hands reproduced in white statuary marble—were brought out of obscurity to grace papier-mâché tables. Blue or white glass cornucopia vases terminating in gilt bronze hands, with ornamented cuffs and rings, were more sought after than similar examples with stags' heads or conventional scrolls, though the stags' heads in particular were also popular. Victorian pinchbeck sets of brooches and earrings representing hands—"Pinchbeck star rises again", declared *Vogue* in 1935—were reproduced as costume jewelry and their popularity inspired Cartier's hand brooches.

The basis of many Surrealist paintings was the juxtaposition of disparate objects to induce in the spectator a sense of unease. To accentuate the incongruity of such an alliance the objects concerned were delineated with a meticulous technique which left the

body, as an element in their paintings or sculptures, as had the group of Herold, Breton, Tanguy and Brauner in their joint "exquisite corpse" drawings. In their case the hand was used to give a shock effect, unlike the more sentimental and purely decorative treatment in the nineteenth century. In 1931 the American edition of *Harper's Bazaar* showed a photograph of a group of hand-ornaments dating from 1850 and later, which were described in the caption as "Pale hands you'll love! They are seventeenth-, eighteenth-, nineteenth-century but all of them as Victorian in feeling as antimacassars and hassocks." Similar hand-ornaments of the white alabaster-like porcelain invented by Bennington in 1852, made at the Copeland and Minton factories and called "Parian" ware, or of the Irish Belleek ware originated about 1860 and covered with an iridescent glaze, were eagerly sought in junk shops or street markets and could be had for a few shillings. Hands holding shells, detachable trumpet vases or vases in the shape of buds or flowers were ideal containers for the small posies of mixed flowers which

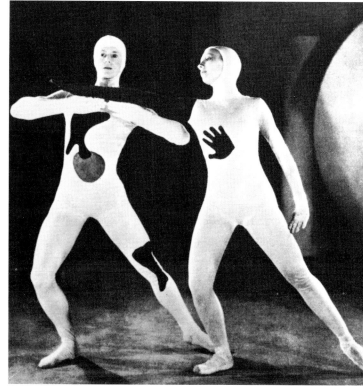

beholder in no doubt as to their identity and all the devices used by the *trompe l'œil* painters of the seventeenth and eighteenth centuries were once more brought into use. This in turn led to a reawakening of interest in the work of artists long neglected, even despised, but now found to have the same hallucinatory and often sinister qualities to be found in canvases by Salvador Dali, René Magritte or Pierre Roy, whose paintings were used for a number of covers for *Vogue*. The tortured landscapes of Salvator Rosa, the feverish portraits of demented clerics and gipsies by Alessandro Magnasco, the fantastic architecture dissolving into a livid light against black skies painted by the mysterious Monsu Desiderio—these were all described by William Gaunt in *Bandits in a Landscape*, published in 1936. Discriminating collectors with a taste for the bizarre were searching for examples of their work and, like Arthur Jeffress, putting them in places of honour in rooms furnished with silver-lacquered Venetian or Charles X furniture. Canvases

Far left: "L'Ultra-Meuble" by Kurt Seligmann, shown at the Paris Surrealist Exhibition in 1938.

Left: Pas de deux from *Jeu d'Enfants*, with sets and costumes designed by Joán Miró, 1932. The dancers were Roland Guérard and Lubov Rostova.

Above: Study of hands, solarized photograph by Man Ray, 1932.

Right: Photographic still-life with plaster hand by Edward McKnight Kauffer, about 1935.

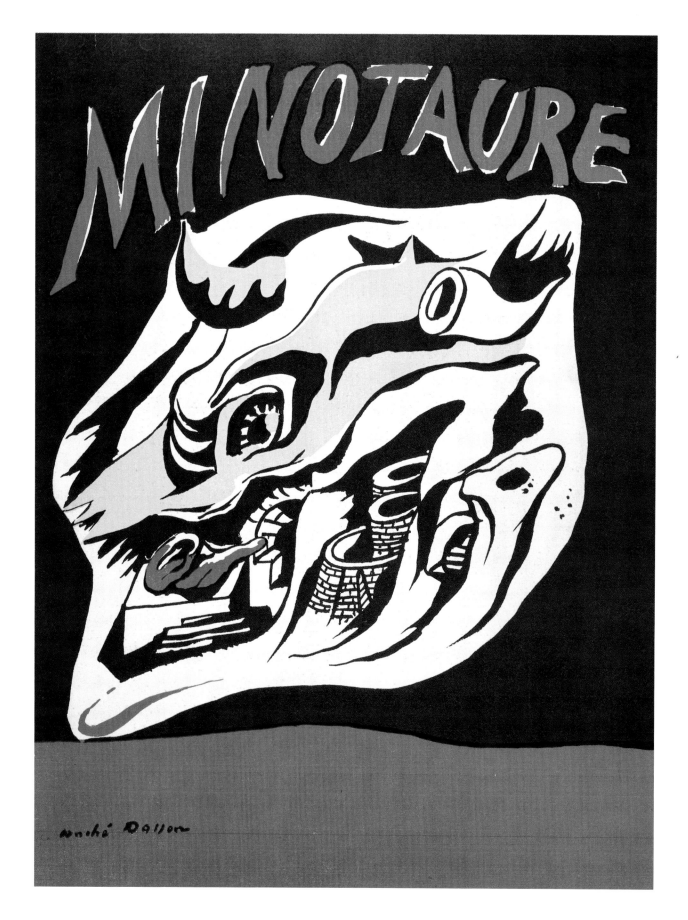

Above: Dress clip by Cartier, about 1937; there were several versions, with the hand in ebony, or red or white coral, and the rose either golden or in carved coral.

Left: Minotaure cover by André Masson, 1939.

by Giuseppe Arcimboldo representing the four seasons, the four elements or the senses, and composed of personages constructed from flowers, vegetable shells or books and paintings which had originally graced the cabinets of curiosities of sixteenth-century Hapsburgs, now re-emerged from obscurity as decorative accompaniments to carved wood blackamoors or Victorian papier-mâché furniture.

The painter Peter Rose Pulham created a series of photographs in a vein of romantic Surrealism which were used as advertisements in fashion magazines by the distinguished couturier Victor Stiebel. He made fashion photographs in the same vein and produced portraits of artists in Paris around 1936 to 1938.

AMERICAN "PRIMITIVES"

Throughout the thirties American collectors had been increasingly interested in the paintings and artefacts of the early years of the United States. These "primitives", who were sometimes skilled in execution but more often painted with more enthusiasm than technique, had an appealing quality of freshness combined with intensity of feeling. In 1935, by chance, the work of a hitherto forgotten painter emerged from the shadows. Alfred Frankenstein tells the story in *After the Hunt*. Edith Halpert, the director of the Downtown Gallery in New York, was offered a painting called *The Faithful Colt* which, in addition to its masterly handling of *trompe l'œil* technique, had the quality of suggesting hidden implications, of arousing speculations. William Hartnett, the creator of this painting, had emerged from an obscurity which, though brief in terms of time (he died in 1892), was profound. Other examples of Hartnett's work were discovered, and by patient scholarship the facts of his life established. The work of a number of imitators also came to light; in fact, it was revealed in time that there had been a school of painters in *trompe l'œil*, highly individual and intent on creating more and more convincing illusions. These in turn influenced many young painters, decorative artists and illustrators.

8
PERIOD REVIVALISM

Evelyn Gardner, in an article entitled "Forward to Neo-Victorianism" published in a 1937 issue of *Harper's Bazaar*, reflected on the increasing tendency to collect the artefacts of the nineteenth century, commenting that "there is one important thing to bear in mind when you decide to follow the fashion and furnish your flat in the neo-Victorian manner and that is *now* is the time to buy these Victorian objects . . . soon prices will soar and those with slender incomes will find that neo-Victorianism is not for them." The trend was not, in the opinion of the writer, a wholesale return to the modes or manners of the Victorian period but rather, in fashion and in furnishing, a judicious mingling of old and new. "The modern young woman . . . has not turned herself into a Victorian, she has decided to become more feminine," and being "bold and adventurous and having filled her flat with glass and steel furniture, she realizes that it will make an excellent setting for the Victorian decorative objects which she was taught in her childhood to despise. There, amongst the straight lines and simplicity of the furniture, the shell flowers

Left: "Victorian" sitting room, decorated by John Fowler in about 1938. The modern white and grey wallpaper served as a foil for the brilliant pink, green, blue, purple and yellow in the Victorian carpet. The glazed chintz curtains, with their elaborately swagged pelmet, and the roller blind printed to simulate a Venetian blind, were modern, but genuine buttoned armchairs, settees and gilt gesso tables were easy to find and inexpensive.

which have lingered so long in dark corners or have been covered by the dirt and dust of the lumber room will look their best." Among "the many beautiful and amusing Victorian objects for us to choose from", the author cites glass ships; embroidered cushions—"definitely amusing"—which as they are "all exceedingly funny and their colours being strong and determined are particularly suited to the modern room"; Victorian glass pictures and wool pictures which "should always be massed together"—a suggestion which in itself is an indication of the changing tastes, and papier-mâché boxes, trays and desks which have "an air of determined usefulness . . . they look out of place as mere ornaments . . . they must be used."

It has come to be accepted that the first sign of a new interest in Victoriana was the result of Lytton Strachey's two biographies *Eminent Victorians* (1918) and *Queen Victoria* (1921). Strachey's original approach to his subjects and his imaginative renderings of the atmosphere of the nineteenth century made him a celebrity overnight and, incidentally, drew the attention of young intellectuals with artistic leanings to the background details of Strachey's subjects. Harold Acton, later to become an eminent biographer of more bizarre personalities, gives an account in his *Confessions of an Aesthete* of the cult of Victoriana which infiltrated Oxford in the early twenties as a reaction against the cult of the 1890s which was still a "faint but flickering tradition". The wan ghosts of Beardsley and Wilde and the echoes of the Grosvenor Gallery received their intimations of oblivion when Harold Acton painted his rooms in Meadow Buildings lemon-yellow and filled them with Victorian bric-à-brac, artificial flowers and fruit, and a collection of paper-weights "imprisoning bubbles that never broke and flowers that never faded". Evelyn Waugh remembers Harold Acton collecting Victoriana when John Betjeman was still a schoolboy rubbing brasses, but does not mention the Acton wardrobe of Victorian-style clothes or the broad trousers which were the originators of the "Oxford bags" of the twenties. The Hypocrites Club was closed as a result of a fancy-

A corner of the study at Wilsford Manor, Wiltshire, decorated by Stephen Tennant with the collaboration of Syrie Maugham, photographed in about 1938.

dress party at which Robert Byron appeared too realistically as Queen Victoria, an occurrence which led to the banning of a proposed "Early Victorian Exhibition" organized by Harold Acton with an illustrated catalogue by Lytton Strachey. Banned too was a Queen Victoria ballet. This new enthusiasm for the nineteenth century was not, of course, confined to a coterie of undergraduates at Oxford. Harold Acton on another occasion mentioned the mingled baroque and Victorian decorations of Osbert Sitwell's house in Carlyle Square when he visited it soon after the first performance of *Façade* in 1931.

This tentative revival of the Victorian style might have flickered out as the result of being confined to a comparatively small circle whose interests would have transferred to some other exoticism when its appeal had begun to pall. It so happened, however, that in the early thirties two circumstances combined to spread and to strengthen it. One was the financial effect of the Depression, the other the paucity of contemporary idioms of ornamentation.

For in certain circles the tendency to ornamentation was apparent even in the early thirties. There were many who emphatically disagreed with the statement of H. S. Goodhart-Rendel, the vice-president of the British Art and Industry Exhibition, that "a fondness for ornament is no more readily acknowledged by refined persons than a fondness for gin, and the natural appetite of the unrefined for pretty patterns is represented as a weakness requiring drastic methods of cure." They were as unashamed in their preference for ornament as in their fondness for gin and in the absence of a popular contemporary ornamented style their only recourse was to that of a past period. Antiques of the sixteenth and seventeenth centuries were beyond the means of most people wanting an original and even slightly outrageous decor. In a period of financial stress it was necessary for interior decorators, artists and anyone even remotely connected with the arts to stand out as possessing adventurous taste and to own an apartment which would be talked about and possibly even photographed for one of the magazines specializing in interior decoration or society gossip. At the same time the elements of such a decor had to be cheap and to a

Right: Studio at Broadcasting House designed by Dorothy Warren Trotter, early 1930s; elsewhere the decorations were distinctly Modernist (below).

certain extent it became permissible to boast of how little one had paid for a chair or an ornament. For such people the rediscovery of the artefacts of the nineteenth century, and in particular the Victorian period, came as a godsend.

It was most welcome also to those decorators, and there were a number of them, who quite early in the decade had begun to realize that it was not altogether in their own interests to encourage their clients to indulge in the fashion for Modernist rooms. The return to a period style produced not only more spectacular results but, more importantly, greater profits. For while Regency and Victorian furniture was very cheap and the decorator could both acquire and install it with the minimum of effort, either period, once installed, called for harmonizing wallpapers, elaborate window treatments and a plethora of ornaments and pictures—and a bigger profit margin.

The earlier Regency had its adherents, especially among those whose aim was an atmosphere of elegance combined with novelty. Particularly popular was wallpaper and fabric with a "Regency stripe", a decorative motif of dubious authenticity which after the Second World War was to become a hackneyed cliché. As early as 1932 and even in the relentless Modernism of Broadcasting House, London, there could be found an essay in the Regency manner. Designed by Dorothy Warren Trotter, the basement studio was given an intimate atmosphere by means of a false window screened by pale green curtains with a swagged pelmet, white-painted bookcases, pale terracotta pink walls and Regency furniture, including an armchair formerly in Arnold Bennett's collection. The colour illustration of this room featured in *The Architectural Review* showed the contrast between this decorative scheme and the functional austerity of the other studios with their steel furniture and Modernistic carpets by Marion Dorn.

Victorian furniture and ornaments, however, could be found at even lower prices than their Regency counterparts. The full-blooded exuberance characteristic of the artefacts of the mid nineteenth century was in sufficient contrast to the monotone sleekness of Modernism to have a degree of shock value which gave an added zest to the sensation of being able to appreciate a style still out of favour with the majority.

Junk shops and street markets were crammed with the artefacts manufactured in vast quantities in the mid nineteenth century. Since the end of the war the big houses of the middle classes, formerly inhabited by one family, had been sold or split into several apartments—an increasing trend as money grew scarcer and domestic help beyond most people's means—and their contents dispersed. Those with "more taste than money" (to quote a description appearing in *Vogue* during the thirties) discovered the Caledonian Market in North London and the Marché aux Puces in Paris to be full of nineteenth-century treasures at derisory prices. The Caledonian Market, or to give it its proper name The Islington Cattle Market, was open on Tuesday and Friday for the sale of second-hand objects, the dealers occupying the enclosures reserved for livestock on the other days. A certain number of stalls were under cover but these were mostly occupied by silver dealers whose stocks were, it was said, of dubious origin. The real bargains were to be found on the cobblestones—the market was affectionately known as "the Stones"—and there, for a few shillings or even pence, could be found an assortment of good and bad articles from all periods and countries. Victoriana was particularly abundant, ranging from original Worth dresses, jet and pinchbeck jewelry to complete suites of parlour furniture in rosewood or papier-mâché, often with the original Berlin woolwork coverings embroidered with lush pink roses or beadwork lilies.

Support for the neo-Victorian trend came also from another direction. Throughout the twenties the majority of picture dealers in London and Paris had thriven on the export of old masters to the United States and particularly on the sale of eighteenth-century portraits by Romney, Gainsborough and Reynolds, for which there was an insatiable demand. Many dealers relied entirely on this export trade and did not consider it necessary to hold exhibitions of contemporary painters, which in many cases entailed considerable work with little material profit either to the gallery or the artist. The gain from the sale of one old master could amount to more than that from a year's showings of even established living artists. This flourishing state of affairs was suddenly ended in December 1929 and many dealers found themselves in the position of having a number of valuable paintings in the United States which had not been paid for and which the clients were in no position ever to pay for. In addition the majority of their clients, if not actually ruined, were in no mood to invest any further in unnecessary luxuries. Thus many galleries found themselves facing ruin and bankruptcy.

The Leicester Gallery, however, had for a long time pursued the policy of holding regular exhibitions of contemporary English and French painters, and by maintaining high standards of quality in their shows had built up a faithful clientele. As they were not so dependent on the export of old masters, the gallery was in a better position than most to weather the dreary years of depression which lay ahead, although the chances of selling expensive paintings remained small. Oliver Brown, a director of the Leicester Gallery, sensed that the interest in Victoriana might appeal to his clients, who could not resist the appeal of an attractive painting provided that the price was reasonable. He collected together examples of the work of a number of painters who flourished in the Victorian period, whose names had been almost forgotten, about whom little was known and, in consequence, whose paintings and drawings could be found at a very small price. An exhibition of drawings by Constantin Guys, a French artist with many connections with England, was extremely successful and every drawing was sold. This was followed in 1933 by the work of James Tissot, another French painter working in England in the 1870s. His canvases, immaculately finished, depicting elegantly dressed women in the charming fashions of the day posed on the decks of yachts were a popular success and were much reproduced in the press. For those who could not afford a Tissot or a Guys there were thousands of Victorian fashion plates available for as little as a few pence each. The paintings of Richard Dadd, whose acute mental disturbance was reflected in the sinister stare common to all his characters and in the fantastic imagery which is seen at its best in *The Fairy Feller's Master Stroke*, Gustave Doré's engravings and illustrations, the paintings of John Martin and those of other minor but fascinating artists helped to swell the interest in Victoriana.

Interest naturally turned to the Victorian narrative paintings and to scenes of everyday life. By the thirties Victorian women's costume was no longer considered hideous or funny and had begun to acquire a period charm. The solid comfort depicted in so many narrative paintings and the crowded clutter of furniture and ornaments which, like the women's dresses, was beginning to be looked at with admiration, were a reminder, at a period of depression and uncertainty, of the security and expansion of middle-class life in England. The fact that underlying the surface of prosperity and cosy warmth depicted in Victorian narrative painting there was an almost limitless area of misery and degradation was as yet unexplored, though hinted at in many paintings. It is possibly too extreme to find an explanation for the Victorian revival of the 1930s in a desire to escape from uncertainty into a past which seemed in retrospect more secure; what is certain is that the elaboration of Victoriana came as a reaction against the starkness of Modernism.

"The Victorian Age Returns" was the heading of an article in *Vogue* in 1931. In *Vogue* circles it had returned already. In another three or four years the fashion had become general, and the Victorian revival was in full swing. However, the reappraisal of Victorian decorative arts was not, of course, endorsed by the advocates of simplicity. John Milne, a member of the executive committee of the British Art in Industry Exhibition, gave voice to a typical view that "to us the Victorian age stands out as a conspicuous example of a period of retrogression" and that "the Great Exhibition of 1851 was the high-water mark of assertive bad taste". As late as 1945, Hayes Marshall, Director of the Decorative Furniture Department at Fortnum and Mason, was of the opinion that "there may be a flashback to 'Victoriana' for a little while, but I do not view this seriously and suggest you restrain your thoughts in this direction. Little furniture of the period is worth a second thought and beyond this reference I wish to forget it." Nevertheless, during the 1930s Mr Marshall's department had stocked numerous pieces of Victorian furniture and ornaments made into lamps.

THE NICHOLAS DU PLANTIER APARTMENT

As a general rule *The Architectural Review* gave prominence to examples of Modernistic interior decoration, but occasionally space was devoted to illustrating a scheme which was of exceptional interest from a decorative aspect. Nicholas du Plantier's apartment featured in 1934 was a portent of the craze for elegant fantasy which conquered Paris during the latter years of the decade, mounting to a climax in 1938. The text accompanying the illustrations was careful to point

The Paris apartment of Nicholas du Plantier, decorated in the early 1930s: the vestibule (*above left*), the bedroom (*below left*) and the hall salon (*below*).

out that the decorations were an example of "period revivalism"—a very different matter from furnishing in period style, something which would not have merited recognition from *The Architectural Review* with its policy of presenting the best of modern furniture and decoration.

Period revivalism—a clumsy title which failed to gain currency—was, in fact, not quite so different from furnishing in a period style as the article suggested, but gave the decorator more freedom to indulge in rather theatrical flights of fancy or to combine genuine antiques with modern pastiches of the same style. Perhaps the most noticable characteristic was a partiality for the neglected periods, for the more decorative furniture of the Biedermeier, Victorian baroque or eighteenth- or nineteenth-century Gothic revival or even ancient Greek styles. The salon of the apartment was planned to give an atmospheric setting for a collection of Etruscan pottery, a Greek marble torso and a classic sculptured head. The obvious clichés of classic columns or key patterns were avoided and the walls and ceiling were painted in a shade of "clouded terracotta". The chairs of oak were of simplified Greek shapes, more a reference to than a copy of those depicted in Greek vase paintings, and the upholstery in rough wool fabric was complemented by thick white fur rugs. In complete contrast was the bedroom where the walls, equally plain, were painted rose cyclamen and draped with white transparent fabric. Two Second Empire chairs, one of black papier-mâché inlaid with mother-of-pearl flowers, the other upholstered and deep-buttoned in satin, formed a contrast with the long, low dressing table, square and modern in design and covered with mirror.

T. H. ROBSJOHN-GIBBINGS

In marked contrast was a room designed by T. H. Robsjohn-Gibbings to serve as a showroom. This decorative scheme intended to break with both the contemporary concepts of Modernism and the accepted "period" associations. It featured "klismos" chairs of waxed birch and a mosaic floor inspired by the fourth-

century BC example in the House of Good Fortune at Olynthos near Salonika.

The scheme aroused considerable interest when it opened in 1936. Its creator had first arrived from England in 1929 to assist Joseph Duveen in his vast enterprise of transferring eighteenth-century England across the Atlantic—an undertaking which suffered a severe check after the Wall Street Crash. The rich diet of period reconstruction imposed upon anyone connected with the Duveen firm came to be antipathetic to Robsjohn-Gibbings—as can be seen in his book, *Goodbye Mr Chippendale*—and it was towards the combined simplicity and elegance of classical Greek furniture and ornament that he turned for inspiration. The so-called timelessness of the majority of Modernist designs was in his view a fallacy—time has proved the accuracy of this opinion—and the doctrinaire adherence to stark, straight outlines and unornamented surfaces a retrograde step. The search for beauty could encompass a graceful curve or a subtly moulded out-

line to a support. The form of his 1936 chair owes more than a little to Greek prototypes, but the elegant simplicity of its lines makes it one of the classics of modern chair design.

THE HELENA RUBINSTEIN APARTMENT

Few decorative schemes received more publicity in France, England and the United States than that for the residence of Helena Rubinstein in Paris. Situated on the Ile St Louis, the seventeenth-century house at 26 Quai de Béthune had been modernized by the distinguished architect Louis Süe, one of the leading exponents of the Art Deco manner. Mme Rubinstein was an inveterate collector with a wide appreciation of different styles, and being a "princess of industry" had the means to gratify her taste and knowledge.

Above left: Deep-buttoned furniture by Robsjohn-Gibbings, part of his decoration in 1937 of Mrs J. O. Weber's house, the Casa Encantada, in Bel-Air, California.

Left: Console table in carved Canadian birch by Robsjohn-Gibbings, made by the Peterson Studios for the Casa Encantada, 1937.

Right: Room decorated by Louis Süe for Helena Rubinstein's house, about 1938.

Very little seems to have remained of the interior structure of the house after its adaptation to form a setting for her collection, and certainly it is doubtful if without extensive alterations the ancient structure could have supported the weight of the pool with illuminated fountains containing over four thousand gallons of water which was placed on the roof, alongside a small dining room with walls of mirror brick and a glass ceiling.

The task facing Louis Süe, that of creating settings for collections of antique furniture and contemporary works of art, was no easy one, but there were few who could have solved it more satisfactorily. As early as 1911 Mme Rubinstein had demonstrated her prowess as a collector when she entered Paterson's Gallery in Bond Street and unhesitatingly purchased the entire exhibition of sculpture by her Polish compatriot Elie Nadelman, a protégé of Leo and Gertrude Stein and according to some critics the original creator of Cubism. Since then her collection of sculpture had been enlarged with works of Brancusi whose "Bird in

Space" was given a special place before a window where it was silhouetted against the church of St Louis-en-l'Ile, Picasso and "anonymous negro and Egyptian artists of primitive persuasion". Selected pieces from this collection were arranged in the entrance hall in company with paintings by Picasso, Dufy and Marie Laurencin: the rugs and upholstery were woven under the direction of Mme Cuttoli and the simple vellum-covered stools and low tables were by Jean-Michel Frank. All the curtains throughout the apartment were designed and woven by Mme Paule Marrot. The dining room was decorated with a set of antique hand-blocked wallpaper by Dufour representing views of Lyons and furnished with Charles X furniture. The most spectacular room, however, was undoubtedly Mme Rubinstein's bedroom, in which all the furniture was veneered in mother-of-pearl, a conception which if not unique—Misia Sert had a number of pieces of similarly treated furniture of the same period, the Second Empire—was more memorable than the occasion for which it was originally created,

Bedroom in Helena Rubinstein's Paris house, about 1938.

Interior by Lady Mendl, late 1930s, showing the theatrical element characteristic of many interiors of the late thirties. The neo-Baroque details are silhouetted against "antiqued" mirror and the alcove, lined with velvet, displays a painting of a ruin. The modern furniture is loosely based on elaborate Italian eighteenth-century originals.

the marriage of the Duc de Montpensier, fifth son of Louis Philippe, and the sister of Queen Isabella II of Spain. To set off this furniture Louis Süe had created a decor of yellow walls and white padded satin decorated with gold cord in diamond patterns.

Helena Rubinstein's apartment was possibly the climax of "une offensive de goût baroque", as it was described by René Charance. Even at a time when fantasy was in vogue she was considered to have reached the limit in these schemes. In one room such disparate elements as a near life-size painted and gilded African woman, a tortured and fretted Indian chair and table, a silver-leaf-finished Italian shell-settee combined with African sculpture and Pavel Tchelitchew's portrait encrusted with sequins, created an appropriate setting for one of the more flamboyant personalities of the time.

BLACKAMOORS

The baroque revival with its emphasis on the decorative rather than the historically accurate brought back into popularity the carved wood figures collectively known as blackamoors. Long out of fashion, these had gathered dust in storerooms, attics or the basements of antique shops where the hopelessly unsaleable objects were banished. The smaller porcelain figures of blacks and Moors, sometimes forming parts of sets representing the four continents, had always been sought after by porcelain collectors, but the larger wooden figures, even if serving a practical purpose, could find no room in Art Nouveau, Art Deco or Modernist schemes.

This new fashion was undoubtedly of Parisian origin and appears to have begun about 1933. Before long a number of exclusive Paris decorators, including Jean-Michel Frank and Serge Roche, were displaying blackamoors in their different postures. Carlos de Beistegui's Dresden copy of a blackamoor figure was one of the most spectacular. A few of the blackamoors, mainly in the form of *torchères*, dated from the eighteenth century, but the majority had been made in the 1860s and 1870s, though these too were generally attributed to the earlier period. These painted and gilded wooden figures, often life-size, were of Italian origin and depicted black males and females, though a less popular type had bearded Moorish features. Half-concealed under carved wooden draperies, they supported console tables; dressed in gilded and painted costumes, they held small trays for visiting cards; small figures supported stools, while there was a type much sought after which represented acrobats, standing on their hands and supporting a tray on the soles of their feet or crouched in an uncomfortable posture holding up the upholstered seat of a stool on their feet.

Below: Coco Chanel, wearing one of her own designs, photographed in her Paris apartment by Cecil Beaton, 1935–37.

Above: Neo-baroque interior of about 1937, an assemblage of the favourite motifs used in this type of decoration. The blackamoor is of carved and painted wood; the buttoned settees are covered in felt and trimmed with cotton fringe; a palm-tree ornament sets off the white-painted commode; real shells, painted to match the walls, surround the mirror, and the curtains are boldly striped. The simplicity of the mantel surround and the absence of mouldings suggest that before the neo-Baroque fashion the room may have had a starker appearance.

This fashion, which quickly spread to England and America, inevitably led to the appearance of many more or less convincing fakes—a trade which still exists though, in the present climate of opinion, the fashion has more or less passed and the figures are now referred to as "Nubians". Cases were known of carved wood figures of angels from Italian baroque churches which were recarved and painted to simulate blacks to meet the demand, and one collector proudly installed a pair of life-size black acrobats as supports in the inglenook of the dining room in a fake Tudor cottage—ignorant of the fact that his apparent carved wood eighteenth-century blackamoors were in fact plaster and had been made less than a year previously for a window display in a department store. The

Right: Dress clip or brooch by Cartier, about 1937, reputedly based on an eighteenth-century Venetian model.

blackamoor theme was continued in jewelry. In the eighteenth century a favourite black slave would wear a collar with the name of his owner engraved upon it—the pathetic story of such a slave was told by Constance Wright in her novel *Silver Collar Boy*, published in 1934 with Rex Whistler's illustrations. Now the position was reversed—a fashionable woman would wear at her neck Cartier's gold, onyx and enamel clip of a black's turbanned head. The design of the clips or brooches was reputed to have been based on an original eighteenth-century Venetian model. A passable imitation of the blackamoor head was mass-produced in gilded metal with the face painted black and the turban white, with smaller versions as ear clips.

DECORATIVE MOTIFS

Among the exhibits shown by Serge Roche in 1934 was a decorative plaster lamp standard modelled as a conventionalized palm tree—the indirect lighting concealed in the spreading leaves at the apex. In design it resembled eighteenth-century prototypes by Delafosse, Roubo and Blonde among others, and may have been directly cast from an architectural fragment of the period. A complete table, also of plaster, with a top supported by two truncated palm sprays, bore a close family resemblance to Roche's lamp standard and appeared in a number of drawing rooms in France and England, where it was incorporated into schemes of decoration by Syrie Maugham.

Another eighteenth-century motif to come back into fashion was the sea-shell, the curves and convolutions of which were among the basic ingredients of the rococo style. In a number of cases the derivation from eighteenth-century sources was obvious, for instance in the carved and painted furniture modelled as over-scaled shells, conceived with a gusto which an earlier period might have found excessive but which now enjoyed a vogue. Eighteenth-century Venetian chairs of silvered wood with seats and backs carved as flat shells and the legs representing mollusc-encrusted stalactites were once again sought after as decorative pieces and about 1938 Arthur Jeffress decorated a bedroom in his country house with a collection of silvered furniture in this style, combined with mural paintings in sanguine monotone by the author.

Below: Plaster floor lamps in the form of trees, attributed to Serge Roche, mid 1930s.

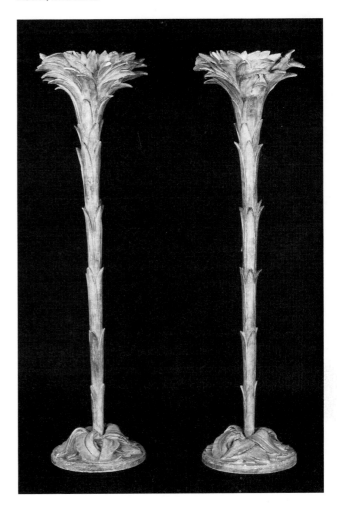

9

FASHION

The trends in interior decoration were closely paralleled through the thirties by women's clothes, especially in the case of the models designed in Paris. In the same way that the Depression influenced interior design, so the luxury trades in which Paris, in the thirties as much as the twenties, was the undisputed arbiter of taste, reflected the economic stresses of the early years of the decade. Fabrics hitherto regarded as unsuitable were used for evening dresses, and models in cotton in its various forms were shown by the younger designers like Chanel and Schiaparelli. Similarly, cotton ticking or the blue and white striped fabric used for butchers' aprons was made into curtains or used for upholstery as a substitute for silk or damask—a false economy in actual fact as the cost of labour involved in making up the curtains remained the same whatever the material, and clients were often disconcerted to find that their new curtains made from a fabric costing a mere two shillings or so a yard did not after all work out at a tenth of the price of a more expensive fabric.

The fashion for frankly artificial jewelry which Chanel had been instrumental in launching during the twenties became a necessity rather than a diverting whim. The Colonial Exhibition held in Paris in 1931 led to a spate of barbaric heavy jewelry made of gilded or silvered metal combined with enamelling, carved from horn—a favourite material of Colette Guedon, the designer for Au Printemps—tortoiseshell or artificial substances like galalith and catalin, the forms and decorations being drawn from African prototypes and blended with Cubism. The *avant-garde* obsession with machinery could be seen in such an example as a Jean Fouquet bracelet of ebonite rings enclosing chromium-plated ball-bearings, the heads of the connecting screws being left unconcealed.

On a more sumptuous scale, Maubousson and Van Cleef and Arpels were designing jewelry influenced by "ornaments strange and exotic from darkest Africa", to quote from a feature article with coloured drawings by Charles Martin in *Harper's Bazaar* for August 1931. Here yellow, red and white gold, ivory and carved coral were combined in a necklace, earrings and clip while Maubousson created an even richer effect by the use of gold, platinum, blue enamel, black enamel and brilliants in a parure of a brooch and necklace.

The number of clients rich enough to indulge in such elaborate jewelry was strictly limited, however, and even these were cautious about spending money at a time when the general economy was in such a precarious condition. The simplicity of the fashions of 1930 reflect not only the trend to elimination of ornament but also the need for economy. The boyish look of the mid-twenties with its short, straight dresses was already on the wane by the end of the decade—skirt lengths had dropped by 1930 to a generally accepted

Left: Lee Miller in a dress by Jean Patou, photographed by George Hoyningen Huene in 1931. The jewelry is by Van Cleef and Arpels, and the furniture by Jean-Michel Frank.

"The Ballroom of the Dorchester Hotel", 1931, by Fortunio Matania, an extremely popular illustrator of the twenties and thirties whose historical reconstructions, rendered with great accuracy of detail, were much in demand by popular magazines. The Dorchester Hotel was started in 1930 and built at the rate of one floor a week. Its opening was celebrated by the publication of a special book, containing a short story by Michael Arlen, "A Young Man Comes to London", and folding colour plates showing the demolition of the old Dorchester House and the construction of the new building.

Right: Pendant in gold, aventurine and onyx, designed by Gérard Sandoz in 1928–30 and exhibited at the Pavillon de la France Metropolitaine, at the Exposition Coloniale in Paris, 1931.

Below: Diamond dress clip by Cartier, late 1930s. Thousands of dress clips were made in the period 1935–38, in materials ranging from rubies, emeralds, sapphires and diamonds to paste and various forms of plastic.

level of fourteen inches (35 cm) off the ground for day wear, twelve inches (30 cm) for afternoon wear and ankle-length for evening. "We have finished with angularity and hardness," declared a fashion writer in 1930. The new soft yet streamlined look was achieved by intricate bias-cutting around the hips and thighs, the waistline, where marked, being either in the natural position or lower according to taste and the bust unemphasized in the evening, while the bodices of day dresses had "scarfs, jabots, revers, girdles and bows, all of these frequently merging softly one into the other". Hair was set close to the head, covered in daytime by small hats of draped felt or worked straw, no longer worn down to the eyebrows as in the twenties but revealing the forehead on one side and caught by a jewelled clip. These clips, either single or in pairs which could be combined to make a brooch, were absolutely essential as an ornament to any well-dressed woman during the thirties, and innumerable models were designed—many, Depression or no Depression, in real diamonds set in the newly fashionable platinum or white gold, and of course even more in paste. One can only admire the ingenuity of designers in contriving endless variations upon the same theme.

Furs were of the short-haired variety and breitschwanz, shaved caracal, lamb, beaver and astrakhan were treated to be supple enough to be used as knots on collars or bows on coats and capes.

1930–1931

The sleek look considered desirable in 1930, entailing the use of smooth fabrics—crêpe, satin or facecloth —and the lack of any ornamental detail beyond the often intricate cutting of the fabric, was not for the majority of women an easy fashion to follow. The clinging evening dresses shaped to the figure by bias-cutting, a technique introduced by Madelaine

Below: The couturier Charles James adjusting the brim of one of his felt hats, photographed by Cecil Beaton.

Above: The couturier Alix, a portrait in lacquer by Jean Dunand, 1933.

Vionnet, were mercilessly revealing and required a perfect Junoesque figure and a minimum of underwear, unless the lines of the dress were to be spoiled by bulges and too many shoulder straps. In the following year a more accommodating look began to appear and the first signs of the direction in which fashion was to develop during the next ten years can be detected. "Women will, at last, wear clothes worthy of the name," was the relieved comment of a journalist in this year, forecasting the more individual approach to fashion design characteristic of the decade. This was owing to a variety of reasons: the economic conditions, the gathering momentum towards period revivalism and the fiercer competition for an entirely different clientele. The days had vanished when Paul Poiret could snub a rich client whom he considered not to have been sufficiently appreciative of his creations. Although there were still patrons able to order a new wardrobe every season, the wholesale buyers from abroad and the editors of fashion magazines were becoming more necessary to the career of any couturier and particularly important to the new couturiers. Maggy Rouff, daughter of Drécoll, opened her salon in 1929, as did Bruyère, who had worked with Jeanne Lanvin; Mainbocher opened in 1930, Nina Ricci in 1931, and Alix, a former sculptress and pupil of Premet, two years later. Chanel, of course, had been well established for some considerable time, while Schiaparelli had opened her doors at 21 Place Vendôme, the former house of Cheruit, in 1929. Chanel's ascendancy as a designer for the young was unchallenged, though Schiaparelli's flair for publicity and exploitation of novelty had led her to be considered by many contemporary journalists as more in tune with the period.

1932–1933

The smaller collections shown in Paris in 1932 were a sign of the times and equally significant were the individual efforts of the couturiers to express their ideas of the development of fashion. While Molyneux dropped the waistline to the hips and Schiaparelli raised it to just under the bust, Worth and Lanvin left it in its natural position. Mainbocher made tentative efforts to emphasize the bust, Worth plunged with enthusiasm into military effects of epaulettes, brass buttons and small peaked caps, and Patou designed variations on the diagonal line. Striped fabrics and elaborate buttons were prevalent but the most marked feature of the year was the preponderance of white, from evening dress to beachware.

In 1933 a fashion correspondent made the observation that the chic new word was "amusing . . . no longer is anything a 'bore'". It was too early for this to be taken as a significant pointer to the lessening of the Depression, which was in fact to linger for nearly

two years more, but as a word it was useful to describe the vagaries of fashion. Another word constantly used by caption writers until 1939 was "romantic"—increasingly popular as the neo-Victorian trend gathered momentum. It was applied to the "Empress Eugénie" hat popular in 1931–32, a small hat resembling a flat bowler, decorated with a sweeping ostrich feather and worn tilted over one eye. Originally of hatters' velvet with a thick luxuriant feather, it was copied in cheaper versions until it finally became a skimpy travesty of the original and then suddenly disappeared as a fashion.

Small hats continued to be worn in 1933, generally on the side of the head, and as many variations on the fez, the beret and the stocking cap were devised as there were on the diamond clip. Schiaparelli's stocking cap proved so popular that the design was pirated in America and in her autobiography she describes how tired she became of seeing it everywhere "until one day it winked at her from the bald head of a baby in a pram. That day she gave the order to her salesgirls to destroy every single one in stock, to refuse to sell it and never to mention it again."

Shoulders began to be accentuated, raglan sleeves were revived, particularly by Charles James, an inspired master of the intricate cut. Three-quarter length "swagger" coats and tunics for dresses were introduced, the mid-calf skirt length and natural waist remaining standard through all the collections. Silver fox—another thirties motif—appeared both as trimming for coats or jackets or more often as a separate fur used singly or doubly. Black monkey-fur was also used and reappeared in collections throughout the thirties, but somehow it never caught on and its decorative possibilities found little response.

1934–1935

It is perhaps an oversimplification to select one evening dress out of the thousands designed in Paris in 1934 as being particularly significant, but in retrospect the Marcel Rochas model, full-skirted, its minimal bodice decorated with a whole stuffed seagull, stands out as a portent of the quasi-Surrealist fantasy which

was to become increasingly noticable until 1939. The clinging bias-cut dresses of three or four years before were giving way to fuller skirts with the waistline clearly defined and the silhouette of day and evening clothes was becoming increasingly diversified. The trend of accentuation of the shoulders was even more marked in coats and dresses, either by padding or decorative motifs such as the cartridge-pleating favoured by Schiaparelli, and hats grew larger to balance the often excessive width of the shoulders.

Much publicity was given in this and the following year to a new fashionable accessory—the *minaudière*. At a time when a long dress was still considered essential for the theatre, dances or dinner parties, the well-dressed woman had to have several evening dresses in her wardrobe. To solve the prob-

Left: Vogue cover design by Georges Lepape, 1934.

Below: Sketch by René Gruau of a hat by Erik, 1934.

Above right: Wedding dress by Mainbocher, 1937.

Right: "Evening Extravaganza", a black faille evening coat by Molyneux, illustrated by Eric for *Vogue*, 1939.

lem of finding an evening bag that would harmonize with all these, Van Cleef and Arpels invented a rigid metal box with compartments for cigarettes, powder, lipstick, money, etc., the exterior finished in lacquer, engine-turned gold or silver and even chromium plate. This was oddly named after a French adjective meaning simpering, affected or lackadaisical, though the compact planning of the interiors of these boxes should have earned the praise in England of the disciples of "fitness for purpose". The *minaudière* was at first sold exclusively in England by Asprey's at prices around £70, but was soon copied in different versions by other jewellers.

Below: Evening dress and stole by Piguet, photographed by Constantin Joffé in the mid 1930s.

Above: Silver *minaudière* by Cartier, about 1937.

Right: Schiaparelli's "lobster" dress, created in collaboration with Salvador Dali in 1937, shown here worn by Mrs Wallis Simpson in a photograph by Cecil Beaton.

SCHIAPARELLI

In 1935 Schiaparelli opened the first "boutique" in her new premises in the Place Vendôme and "it became instantly famous because of the formula of 'ready to take away immediately'. There were useful and amusing gadgets afire with youth. There were evening sweaters, skirts, blouses and accessories previously scorned by the *haute couture*." As she remarks in her autobiography, "the year 1935 was such a busy one for Schiaparelli that she wonders how she got through it." Schiaparelli numbered among her friends all the *avant-*

garde designers, including Dali, Jean-Michel Frank, Fini and Bérard. Frank was entrusted with the decoration of the boutique, which he transformed into a gilded bamboo birdcage as a setting for displays of the new scent "Shocking" in its bottle (in the shape of a Victorian dress dummy) designed by Léonor Fini, for the house-mascot Pascal, a life-size artist's lay figure in wood, and for an enormous stuffed bear given by Edward James to Salvador Dali, who dyed it shocking pink and put drawers in its stomach.

It was Dali who inspired Schiaparelli most. "Schiaparelli went up into the rarefied skies of her most fantastic imagination and set off cascades of fireworks. Fantasy and ingenuity broke forth, with complete indifference not merely to what people would say but even to what was practical. She sought

Schiaparelli's "shoe" hat, 1937.

only an absolute freedom of expression . . ." In so doing Schiaparelli set a pace of hectic invention which not only reflected the mood of the time but also influenced other couturiers, who might have eyed askance her more exotic flights of fancy but had perforce to provide their clients with something of the excitement she engendered. To elegance she added the attraction of the Surrealistic, the bizarre or the incongruous. In 1932 she had included in her collections a number of dresses with painted decorations by Jean Dunand, but in 1936 a collaboration with Dali, a creator of far more feverish imagination, led to the appearance of an evening dress with the skirt printed with a life-size red lobster with a few green motifs scattered on the bodice to represent parsley. Dali's wish to spatter the dress with real mayonnaise was thwarted, to his intense regret. This dress, in fact extremely pretty, received much publicity in the fashion magazines, as did another Schiaparelli–Dali creation, a black felt hat in the form of a shoe, with a shocking-pink velvet heel, a reversal of function which was entirely in the Surrealist manner. In 1936 Dali drew "The City of Drawers", representing an agonized nude female with a torso composed of a series of half-open drawers and "The Venus de Milo of the Drawers", a plaster cast of the famous statue treated in a similar fashion. Schiaparelli records in her autobiography that "we devised together the coat with many drawers from one of his famous pictures" —much to the pleasure of the fashion writers who approved rather less of another collaborative effort, a hat "resembling a lamb cutlet with white frill on the bone".

The fruits of this collaboration with Dali more than anything else contributed to Schiap's fame for eccentricity, but almost as extraordinary were the embroidered reproductions of Jean Cocteau drawings on evening coats; her scarves and hats of fabric printed by Colcombet with news articles about herself; her use of the hitherto neglected zipper as a decorative feature; her buttons designed by Jean Clement in wood, metal and plastics, buttons representing padlocks,

Right: Dress by Mainbocher, photographed by Horst, 1938.

mouths, butterflies, mermaids, fox-heads and, inevitably, hands—these creations were guaranteed to ensure a constant stream of publicity in the fashion magazines. Schiaparelli refers to Clement in *Shocking Life* as a "a genius in his way, a real French artisan, who would work with such burning love that he was almost a fanatic. He would arrive at the moment when we had given up all hope of having anything to fasten our clothes. There would be a smirk of triumph on his face while he emptied his pockets into my lap, waiting anxiously for a word of praise."

If Schiaparelli did not inaugurate the practice of basing a collection upon a theme, then she was one of the first to do so. Christian Bérard enthusiastically recorded for *Vogue* her "circus" collection with its motifs of sequinned clown hats and short evening coats embroidered with prancing, plumed white horses. A "pagan" collection of simple, clinging classical gowns embroidered with "wreaths and leaves of delicate flowers" and an "astrological" collection with horoscopes, the stars, the moon and the sun glittering at every step, did not, as might have been expected, shock her more conservative clients—who responded with enthusiasm—but in fact gained her many new ones. These collections based on motifs were a boon to the fashion writers who were released from the tedium of discovering trends in the diversity of fashions in the years between 1935 and 1939. Christian

Left: Lamé evening dress by Madelaine Vionnet, 1937. The model, posed in a wheelbarrow with buttoned upholstery by Oscar Dominguez, was photographed by Man Ray.

Above right: Evening dress and short jacket by Maggy Rouff, late 1930s, photographed by Harry Meerson.

Right: Evening dress by Victor Stiebel, 1939, photographed by John French.

Bérard's designs for *La Reine Margot* in 1935, a Winterhalter or a Constantin Guys exhibition, the Balthus designs for *The Cenci*—anything new served as an inspiration for a collection.

THE LATE THIRTIES

Mainbocher's new collection in 1938 was actually a preview of the postwar New Look, with its full skirts over petticoats. A writer in *Harper's Bazaar* described the collection as "significant and prophetic"—a prophecy which in fact was realized only after the Occupation—and while the French found them reminiscent of the illustrations in the Bibliothèque Rose volume of children's stories *Les Malheurs de Sophie*, the American buyers chauvinistically decided they had been inspired by *Little Women*.

The prevailing bias towards period revivalism to be found in interior decorating during the late thirties was reflected in high fashion. The Edwardian period inspired the upswept hair, full skirts and soft pastel colour, but in this case a corresponding influence was

absent from the decor of the house—Art Nouveau was still a sleeping beauty despite Evelyn Waugh's effort to interest the readers of *The Architectural Review* in the work of Gaudi. Balenciaga, newly arrived in Paris as a refugee from the Spanish Civil War, had opened a salon (after a brief unsuccessful sojourn in London) and was reminding Parisiennes of the paintings of Velasquez, using a typically Spanish palette of rich dark colours and a determination to awaken a realization of the elegance of black combined with brown. Patou's collection, influenced by Egyptian mummy wrappings, brought about a charming series of drawings by Bérard but little else, and in London the highly successful and talented theatrical designers working under the name of Motley opened a *salon de couture*, but their first collection, inspired by medieval sources, was considered to adhere too closely to the originals to be chic and came more into the category of fancy dress than fashion. It was, in fact, thirty years ahead of its time.

10
HOLLYWOOD STYLE

Cinemas were the dream palaces of the thirties where moviegoers could find momentary escape from the worries and irritations of everyday life. These dream palaces with their exotic decoration, multi-coloured lighting and soothing music were a prelude to the moment when a warm, comforting darkness enveloped the audience and the gleaming satin curtains swept aside to display the titles of another movie where right triumphed over wrong, true love conquered all and the final embrace of hero and heroine was a guarantee of a lifetime of perfect bliss. For the female members of the audience there was the possibility that, even if their lives could never begin to approximate to that of their favourite stars as shown on the screen or written about in the movie magazines, they could at least wear a frock or a hat similar to that of their idol and by doing so perhaps acquire a morsel of the cool elegance of Myrna Loy, Katharine Hepburn or Norma Shearer. For during the thirties Hollywood and its dress designers began seriously to rival Paris.

The advent of the talkies had brought a new element into Hollywood, an influx of talent from the legitimate theatre. Actors, playwrights and directors

Left: The revolving dance set at the climax of the three-hour musical *The Great Ziegfeld*, 1936, which won an award for its designer Seymour Felix. Such spectacular song and dance numbers had been first created in the early 1930s by Busby Berkeley, who gave his name to the whole genre.

were lured from New York and London to translate successful plays into the new medium and although the many musicals produced in the late twenties and early thirties continued the Hollywood tradition of decorative fantasy, the domestic dramas or drawing-room comedies demanded a more restrained and naturalistic idiom of dress design once the human voice was added. At the same time "certain actresses of great personal chic in private life refused to be dressed like Christmas trees on the films". The talents of new designers, such as Adrian and Howard Greer, were engaged by the major companies to enhance and accentuate the different personalities of the movie stars. It was not an easy assignment. Between the designing of the clothes and the release of the film a period of anything up to a year might elapse, during which time Paris might have dictated a sudden change in silhouette or length. In addition a successful film might be shown for a couple of years or more and it was essential that the leading players should not appear old-fashioned. Thus the influence of Paris came to be disregarded and attempts were made to evolve a style of designing which would appear fashionable but would be at the same time dateless. Yet, by strange coincidence, Paris and Hollywood often appeared to have the same ideas at the same time. Garbo's clothes designed by Adrian for the film *Mata Hari* (1931) had the same accent on broad shoulders as those shown in Paris collections at the time the film was released, and similarly, small pill-box hats appeared at the same time in the French collections

Above: Set design for *Our Dancing Daughters*, 1928, showing early Modernist influences in the furniture and the lighting.

and in the movies. To cut down costs of photography some women's magazines, in particular *Woman and Beauty*, used publicity stills from the Hollywood studios to illustrate articles on fashion, carefully choosing those which most nearly approximated to the latest Paris models, with the added glamour of being able to use the names of currently popular stars. Wholesale manufacturers were quick to exploit the influence of Hollywood fashions and as soon as a film was released the ready-made dress shops were flooded with copies or inexpensive versions of the outfits worn by the star. One London hat shop during the thirties had the idea of placing small cards bearing the names of the current film favourites on each hat displayed, with the result that an extravagant creation might one day be labelled Myrna Loy, the next day Joan Crawford, and on subsequent days Carole Lombard, Greta Garbo, Rosalind Russell, until it was finally sold.

On the other hand, Hollywood's influence on interior decoration was negligible if, in fact, there was any at all. The number of movies with settings in a modern idiom was surprisingly small considering the enormous output from the Hollywood studios. The sets created for musicals like the series starring Fred Astaire and Ginger Rogers, for instance, were so lavishly unrealistic as to be impractical as a source of inspiration. Of the more naturalistic films many were on historical themes set in various periods—these included, of course, the many Westerns—and while the dresses and particularly the hairstyles of the actresses often made few concessions to historical veracity (many an eighteenth-century character or saloon-bar girl in a Western turned her back to the camera to reveal a very obvious zip-fastener), the settings usually showed a considerable degree of period accuracy. Even when it was necessary to provide a modern background suggesting wealth or elegance, the set designers, possibly for the same reasons that the costume designer had to design clothes that avoided any sudden changes of fashion in the world of reality, invariably tended to think in terms of pseudo-eighteenth-century rooms with

anonymous period furniture. This furniture came from the studio store-rooms and could be used over and over again, suitably re-covered in different materials to avoid being recognized—though there were a number of decorative pieces which inevitably became familiar to ardent filmgoers. Strictly contemporary furniture of extreme design was seldom, if ever, used since its practical life would be confined to one film of importance.

This adherence to period decors even in movies set in modern times was to a certain extent reflected in the homes of the stars themselves. An article by Geoffrey Boumphrey in *The Architectural Review* reflected the somewhat patronizing attitude adopted by many in pseudo-intellectual circles toward Hollywood and its products. In this case the homes of some of the leading actresses, whose hospitality presumably Mr Boumphrey had enjoyed, were described with some acidity in an article entitled "Hollywood Party". The Louis XIV dining room of "the world's most famous blonde", admittedly no masterpiece of period reconstruction, earned the comment, "Hollywood has

Right: Fred Astaire and Ginger Rogers on the set of *Top Hat*, 1935.

Contemporary set design for the film *No More Ladies* by Cedric Gibbons, 1935.

Mae West and Mae West has Louis and what has Louis to do with life as lived by Mae West except that it costs a lot of money." The home of Miriam Hopkins, described as a "Ye Olde Worlde Interior", was faintly praised as "on the whole not a bad room—I have seen far worse in the homes of our own artistic intelligentsia", but Ida Lupino's living room was found to be "horridly Victorian—I had thought in my simplicity, that except for the Sitwells, rooms like this one only occurred as accidents in these days." Silvia Sydney committed the unforgivable sin—that is, presumably, unforgivable by the purist contributors to *The Architectural Review* with their passion for plain surfaces—of putting a chintz pattern on the walls of her living room and a different pattern on the chairs and settees, earning the sarcastic comment that she had missed the opportunity for more and different designs on the carpet and lampshades. Another room in Miss Sydney's house, innocuously decorated with an oak dresser and windsor chairs, was dismissed as

"Babes in the Wood" decoration. Mr Boumphrey's scathing comments were directed towards the houses of several other film stars and he concluded, "we have discovered nothing definable or even comprehensible —no one style, that is, nor set of principles on which a style might be based."

Probably he was not invited to the newly decorated house of Gary Cooper designed by Mrs Ernshaw of Elsie de Wolfe, Inc. Elegantly spacious and uncluttered, the rooms were white throughout with touches of pastel tones of pink and yellow; considerable use was made of mirrors, the faceted mirror consoles and plaster palm tree light fittings being designed by Serge Roche of Paris, and of zebra skins. The fireplaces were surrounded by cast-glass bolection mouldings—a motif sometimes used to frame pictures.

ENVOI

There is a tendency to treat the thirties as a forgotten period—an interlude between the frenetic gaieties and excitements of the twenties and the grim realities of the forties and the Second World War. Those who have written on the period have been mainly political writers preoccupied with the growing rise to power of the dictators and the inevitability (with hindsight) of world conflict. But for the majority of people, and perhaps more especially artists and craftsmen, and for the greater part of the decade, the main concern was with the hazards of earning a living during the Depression. Thoughts of war began to take on an aspect of fearful reality only in the last year or two before the actual outbreak of hostilities. Ironically enough it was during those same two or three years before 1939 that the careless extravagance of the twenties briefly reappeared, and with it some of the fantasy and imaginative creativity of the earlier decade.

It is almost impossible to distil the essential flavour of the thirties in the way that one could have done in the twenties—to cite a room, a dress or a decorative object which, despite the changes in fashion, seems to sum up the whole decade. As we have seen, a "typical" thirties room could be strikingly functional and streamlined, an essay in neo-Baroque, weirdly Surrealist, a modernized version of Victoriana, Regency or even classical Greek. It is this diversity of styles that makes the period original and exciting. In the words of the Cole Porter song of the period, "Anything goes".

Interior of the New Victoria Cinema, Westminster, designed by Trent and Lewis in 1930. Described as "a dream-like palace under the sea", it was an imaginative concept which received the dubious distinction of being used by a specialist in abnormal psychology as a textbook example of "folie de grandeur" (his other examples were the architectural projects of Adolf Hitler).

SOURCE BOOKS AND FURTHER READING

SOURCE BOOKS FOR THE FIRST EDITION

Abercrombie, Patrick (ed.), *The Book of the Modern House*, London: Hodder and Stoughton, 1939.

Acton, Harold, *Memoirs of an Aesthete*, London: Methuen, 1948.

Alexandrian, Sarane, *Surrealist Art*, London: Thames and Hudson and New York: Frederick A. Praeger, 1970.

Antoine [Antek Cierplikowski], *Antoine*, New York: Prentice Hall, 1945 and London: W. H. Allen, 1946.

Arlen, Michael [Dikrān Kuyumjian], *A Young Man Comes to London*, London: The Marshalsea Press, 1932.

Art and Industry, London: HMSO, 1932.

Bernard, Oliver P., *Cock Sparrow*, London: Jonathan Cape, 1936.

Binder, Joseph, *Colour in Advertising*, London: The Studio, 1934.

British Art in Industry, illustrated catalogue of the exhibition at Burlington House, London, 1935.

Brown, Oliver, *Exhibition*, London: Evelyn Adams and Mackay, 1968.

Carrington, Noel (ed.), *Design in the Home*, London: Country Life, 1933.

Chase, Edna Woolman and Ilka, *Always in Vogue*, London: Victor Gollancz and New York: Doubleday and Company, 1954.

De Wolfe, Elsie, *After All*, London: William Heinemann and New York: Harper and Brothers, 1935.

Doesburg, Theo van, *Principles of Neo-Plastic Art*, Greenwich, Conn.: New York Graphic Society, 1968 and London: Lund Humphries, 1969.

Dowling, Henry G., *A Survey of British Industrial Arts*, Benfleet, Essex: F. Lewis, 1935.

Eberlein, H. D. and C. van Dyke Hubbard, *Glass in Modern Construction*, New York: Charles Scribner's Sons, 1937.

L'Exposition de Paris, introduction by Albert Laprade, Paris: Librairie des Arts Décoratifs, 1937.

Frankenstein, Alfred, *After the Hunt*, University of California Press, 1953.

Frankl, Paul T., *New Dimensions*, London: Payson and Clarke and New York: Harcourt Brace, 1928.

Gaunt, William, *Bandits in a Landscape*, London: The Studio, 1937.

Gloag, John (ed.), *Designs in Modern Life*, London: George Allen and Unwin, 1934.

Hayes Marshall, H. G., *British Textile Designers Today*, Leigh-on-Sea, Essex: F. Lewis, 1939.

Hayes Marshall, H. G., *Within Four Walls*, Leigh-on-Sea, Essex: F. Lewis, 1948.

Holme, Geoffrey, *Industrial Design and the Future*, London: The Studio, 1934.

Ideal Home Exhibition catalogues, London.

James, Edward, *The Gardener who saw God*, London: Duckworth and New York: Charles Scribner's Sons, 1937.

Jean, Marcel, *Histoire de la peinture surréaliste*, Paris: Editions du Seuil, 1959.

Joel, David, *The Adventure of British Furniture*, London: Ernest Benn, 1953.

Kirstein, Lincoln (ed.), *Pavel Tchelitchev Drawings*, New York: H. Bittner and Co., 1947.

Levy, Julien (ed.), *Eugène Berman*, London and New York: American Studio Books, 1946.

Lurçat, Jean, *Designing Tapestry*, London: Rockcliff, 1950 and New York: Macmillan, 1951.

Meller, S., F. Lewis and E. Entwistle, *A Century of British Fabrics*, Leigh-on-Sea, Essex: F. Lewis, 1955.

Miller, Duncan, *More Colour Schemes for the Modern Home*, London: The Studio, 1938.

Mitford, Nancy, *The Pursuit of Love*, London: Hamish Hamilton, 1945.

Nash, Paul, *Room and Book*, New York: Charles Scribner's Sons, 1932.

Naylor, Gillian, *The Bauhaus*, London: Studio Vista and New York: E. P. Dutton, 1968.

Olivier, Edith, *In Pursuit of Rare Meats*, London: HMSO, n.d.

Patmore, Derek, *Colour Schemes for the Modern Home*, London: The Studio, 1933.

'Plastes', *Plastics in Industry*, London: Chapman and Hall, 1940 and New York: Chemical Publishing Company, 1941.

Poiret, Paul, *My First Fifty Years*, trans. Stephen Haden Guest, London: Gollancz, 1931; and as *King of Fashion: the Autobiography of Paul Poiret*, Philadelphia: J. B. Lippincott, 1931.

Ray, Man, *Self Portrait*, London: André Deutsch and Boston: Little Brown and Co., 1963.

Read, Herbert, *Art and Industry*, London: Faber and Faber, 1934 and New York: Harcourt Brace, 1935.

Roche, Serge, *Mirrors*, London: Duckworth, 1956.

Rose, Muriel, *Artist Potters in England*, London: Faber and Faber and New York: Pitman Publishing, 1955.

Schiaparelli, Elsa, *Shocking Life*. London: J. M. Dent and Sons and New York: E. P. Dutton, 1954.

Sculpture of Elie Nadelman, The, New York: Museum of Modern Art, 1948.

Spry, Constance, *Flowers in House and Garden*, London: J. M. Dent and Sons, 1937 and New York: G. P. Putnam's Sons, 1938.

Studio Year Books of Decorative Art, The, London: The Studio.

Valette, John de la, *The Conquest of Ugliness*, London: Methuen, 1935.

Waldberg, Patrick, *Surrealism*, London: Thames and Hudson, 1965 and New York: McGraw-Hill Book Co., 1966.

IMPORTANT MAGAZINES OF THE PERIOD

L'Amour de l'Art, Paris.
The Architectural Review, London.
Art and Decoration, New York.
Art, Goût et Beauté, Paris.
The Bourneville Works Magazine, Birmingham.
Harper's Bazaar, London and New York.
House and Garden, London and New York.
Modern Publicity, London.
Photography Year Book, London.
The Studio, London.
Town and Country, New York.
Vogue, London, New York and Paris.
Woman and Beauty, London.

FURTHER READING

Ades, Dawn, *Dada and Surrealism Reviewed*, London: Arts Council, 1978.

Barré-Despond, Arlette, *U.A.M.*, Paris: Editions du Regard, 1986.

Bujou, Guy, and Jean-Jacques Dutko, *Printz*, Paris: Editions du Regard, 1986.

Bush, Donald J., *The Streamlined Decade*, New York: Braziller, 1975.

Garland, Madge, *The Indecisive Decade*, London: Macdonald, 1968.

Garner, Philippe, *Twentieth Century Furniture*, New York: Van Nostrand Reinhold, 1980.

Geest, Jan van and Otakar Máčel, *Stühle aus Stahl-Metallmöbel 1925–1940*, Köln: Walter König, 1980.

Hogben, Carol, *British Art and Design 1900–1960*, London: Victoria and Albert Museum, 1983 and Winchester, Mass.: Faber & Faber, 1984.

MacCarthy, Fiona, *All Things Bright and Beautiful*, London: George Allen and Unwin, 1972.

MacCarthy, Fiona, *British Design since 1880*, London: Lund Humphries and Highlands, N.J.: Humanities Press, 1982.

Martin, Richard, *Fashion and Surrealism*, New York: Rizzoli, 1987.

Purser, Philip, *The Extraordinary Worlds of Edward James*, London: Quartet, 1978.

Thirties—British Art and Design before the War, London: Hayward Gallery, 1974.

INDEX